were foun  *Maple-bank* after doned 60-foot ve ast of Bermuda.

## THE CREW DISAPPEARED
from a 20-foot fiber glass boat, *The Vagabond*, which was found by the Swedish ship *Golar Frost*. A boarding party discovered everything on board undisturbed but no sign of the crew. The last entry in the boat's log was July 2, 1969.

## JULY 8, 1969 . . .
### 36-FOOT CRAFT FOUND CREWLESS
between the Azores and Bermuda by the British tanker *Helisoma*. Nothing could be found in the area to explain why the crew had abandoned her.

## JULY 10, 1969 . . . AIR FORCE
### ABANDONS SEARCH FOR CREW
of a deserted 41-foot, 3-hulled yacht, *Teignmouth Electronic*, found between the Azores and Bermuda. The board of inquiry could not come up with any realistic answer to the disappearance of the crew during a period of extremely calm weather.

### *LIMBO OF THE LOST*
An extraordinary book about one of the strangest phenomena of our time—the tiny strip of sea that has swallowed up boats, ships, planes and people without a trace . . .

# LIMBO
# OF THE LOST

*Actual Stories of Sea Mysteries*

*Revised and Expanded*

## By JOHN WALLACE SPENCER

BANTAM BOOKS · TORONTO · LONDON · NEW YORK

A NATIONAL GENERAL COMPANY

RLI: $\dfrac{\text{VLM 10 (VLR 9–11)}}{\text{IL 9–adult}}$

LIMBO OF THE LOST
*A Bantam Book / published by arrangement with*
*Phillips Publishing Company*

*PRINTING HISTORY*
*Phillips edition published June 1969*
Revised and expanded Bantam edition published September 1973
*2nd printing*
*3rd printing*
*4th printing*

*Picture research by Ann Novotny and Rosemary Eakins,*
RESEARCH REPORTS, *New York.*

*Published simultaneously in the United States and Canada*

*Bantam Books are published by Bantam Books, Inc., a National*
*General company. Its trade-mark, consisting of the words "Bantam*
*Books" and the portrayal of a bantam, is registered in the United*
*States Patent Office and in other countries. Marca Registrada.*
*Bantam Books, Inc., 666 Fifth Avenue, New York, N.Y. 10019.*

PRINTED IN THE UNITED STATES OF AMERICA

# Contents

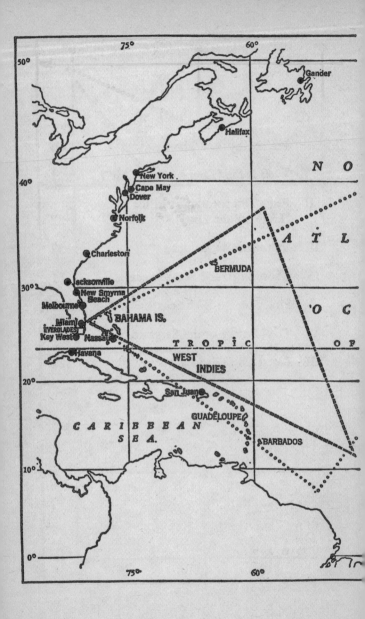

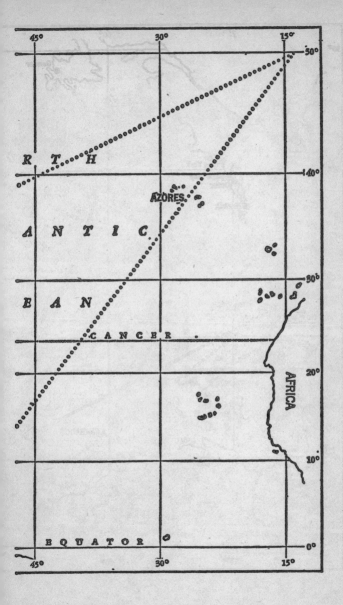

# Preface

The waters of the world know many people. We swim in them. We fish in them. We skim on their surface on water skis. We put on scuba tanks and make brief pilgrimages to coral reefs.

But the seas are selective. They enslave only a few and throw the rest back to the shore. The sea is a goddess of many moods. She can calm and caress you until you are helpless in her embrace, or she can lash out with frightening, destructive power. I have seen and felt her brooding caprice. I have been in awe of her. I have loved her. I have feared her. But my fascination with her deeper mysteries has never faltered. During the last 20 years she has changed me from a kind of diving dilettante to a serious oceanographer.

Actually, almost everyone feels some measure of facination for bodies of water. Some just like to see the sunset reflected in it. Others are curious about what is under the surface. Still others feel a strong unexplainable urge to become a living, breathing part of it.

If we believe the theory that all life began in the sea, we could understand a biological attraction. Take that a step further and we realize that, to all intents and purposes, man has begun a mass migration back to the seas of his birth. In tandem groups, men and women have lived in underwater habitats for up to seven months and efficiently performed useful tasks in what is considered a hostile environment. Two men have plumbed the black depth of the Marianna Trench to 37,800 feet. With the development of scuba tanks (Self Contained Underwater Breathing Apparatus), men and women by the million are exploring the continental shelf. We have begun to mine the seas, farm the seas, and enjoy most of our recreation in the seas.

Can this activity be all biological? All pragmatic? Or do the oceans possess some indefinable extra dimension of fascination and power? Perhaps approaching the spiritual? Or even the extraterrestrial?

Man, today, feeling that he has explored the seas, has become somewhat complacent. He has charted some of the seas, so he knows that beneath the surface are plains and mountains, seaweed forests and arid deserts. He becomes excited at the wealth of food, minerals, and precious ore. He knows that there are volatile volcanoes perhaps a moment away from a cataclysm. Mighty underwater rivers that can change direction at a whim of nature. Seismic waves more than 200 feet high that hurl themselves across the water, destroying everything in their path. Water spouts with the power and fury of a cyclone.

As man has explored the seas and learned about the natural phenomena, he has also gradually become aware, albeit reluctantly, of another facet. The enigmas. The seemingly unfathomable mysteries.

One of the most frustrating, perplexing mysteries of the oceans is most generally known as the "Bermuda Triangle," or, as John Spencer most aptly puts it, the

"Limbo of the Lost." This particular geographic location has become a kind of hole in the water through which have disappeared an unbelievable number of ships and planes. The author presents a well-researched and documented compilation of airplanes and ships that have disappeared in this vast triangle of Atlantic Ocean, which includes such islands as the Azores, Cuba, Jamaica, Haiti, Dominican Republic, Puerto Rico, West Indies, Bahamas, and hundreds of small islands.

Well over a thousand people and more than a hundred planes and ships have mysteriously disappeared there, without a trace—no debris, survivors, lifeboats, or oil slicks. Most often the ships' current position and time of arrival was radioed. After that, nothing. No further communication of any kind.

Hundreds of search planes, ships, and expert personnel have been deployed over thousands of square miles, and yard by yard searches were continued for many days. Sometimes objects were sighted by ship or plane and were thought to be lifeboats or debris, but almost always they turned out to be irrelevant.

The most tantalizing mysteries are those of the derelicts. A classic example is that of the *Mary Celeste,* a brigantine boarded and salvaged by the captain and crew of a British ship. Although her sails were gone and she was listing, she was still navigable. Her cargo was intact. There was not a soul aboard. The ship's navigational gear was missing, which appeared to indicate that the crew had abandoned the ship with careful and thoughtful precautions. So far, no great mystery. Other ships have been caught in severe storms, thought to be sinking, and abandoned by the crew only to survive the storm and sail aimlessly, until picked up and salvaged by another ship. Explainable so far, but the *Mary Celeste* provided a mystery.

Although the navigational equipment was gone, all the seamen's personal effects were left behind. Including objects of value. Not likely. And what happened to the crew? They were never seen or heard from again.

Airplanes too, disappeared without a trace over the "Limbo of the Lost." Violent, clear, air turbulance? A massive thunderhead hidden by a shroud of innocent-appearing clouds? Uneven heating of the water's surface can cause terrifying downdrafts. Natural phenomena that can destroy a plane. But, what happened to the plane after it was ditched? Or the survivors? Or some piece of flotsam that might be considered evidence of a downed airplane?

The mystery is always there, but unless parapsychology quickly develops into an exact science and tells us that the Bermuda Triangle wrecks are the work of some demented, devouring spiritual force, I will have to look to worldly forces and natural phenomena.

In a general way, we know that waves are generated by winds and are an extremely potent force. With strong wind, the waves build in size, continue to travel outside the storm area, and on entering shoal waters rise up and break, expending their energy on the shore or anything else that gets in their way. The dynamics of waves are extremely complex, and we are just beginning to learn about them. We are learning that the topography of the bottom has a vital effect on the behavior of waves, changing them from gentle undulations to raging monsters. We know, too, that in the midst of calm weather and blue skies great heaving walls of waves will arrive on shore. We can imagine what might have happened to any ship in their path. The force and weight of the waves would have crushed it like kindling, spreading the debris over miles of open ocean until it lost all identity. Other potentially destructive waves are referred to as impulsively generated, and they are called seich waves. The most powerful of all mountainous waves is called the seismic wave or *tsunami*. These are created by underwater earthquakes caused by vocanic eruptions or by massive bottom movements resulting from the collapse of faults. Yet another cause of destructive waves is the underwater landslide. Although it is a characteristic of this type to start out as long, low waves, they can, as they pass over the changing topography of the bottom, change into charging giants. These are just a few of the natural possibilities that may have caused the many tragic disappearances in the "Limbo of the Lost." They are logical possibilities based on specific scientific knowledge. Still they seem too meager. After reading Mr. Spencer's unbiased compilation of facts, I have the strong feeling that these logical possibilities are not enough. Part of the puzzle is always missing. I am plagued by the idea that even a long and diligent study of the "Triangle" by experts, would not completely remove the shroud of mystery that persists in the "Limbo of the Lost."

*Jim Thorne*

# I

# What Is the "Limbo of the Lost"?

More than a thousand people and over a hundred ships and planes have mysteriously disappeared in an area of the Atlantic Ocean that I call the "Limbo of the Lost." Ghostly derelicts have been found floundering there, without a clue as to the whereabouts of the crews and passengers.

Tragedies connected to this region continually occur without explanation, without pattern, without warning, and without reason. Extensive air-sea searches have been conducted without the satisfaction of finding enough evidence leading to a realistic answer. The few clues uncovered only add to the mysteries.

The area in question is far from desolate: on the contrary, it appears to go out from Cape May, New Jersey, to the edge of the continental shelf. Following the shelf around Florida into the Gulf of Mexico, it continues through Cuba, Jamaica, Haiti, the Dominican Republic, Puerto Rico, and other islands of the West Indies, and then comes up again through the Bahamas' 20 inhabited islands, plus hundreds of smaller islands too numerous to mention; then up once more to Bermuda with its 360 islands.

Air and sea lanes in the "Limbo" are in constant use both day and night by military, commercial, and private aircraft, ships, and boats. Because sea distances are relatively short, it is safe to surmise that the waters of the "Limbo of the Lost" are virtually covered by craft of one form or another.

Many titles have been hung on this deadly portion of the mid-Atlantic Ocean: "Bermuda Triangle" (writer Vincent H. Gaddis), "The Hoodoo Sea" (writer John Godwin), "Triangle of Death" . . . "Triangle of Tragedy" . . . "Pentagon of Death" . . . "Port of the Missing."

Nobody so far has proclaimed the "Limbo of the Lost" an official danger zone or is anybody apt to. What would happen to the tourist trade?

In spite of radar, radio, modern search technology, life saving apparatus, and speed, man and his machines have and will continue to disappear. Whatever hovers over the "Limbo of the Lost" is responsible for the stranger-than-fiction stories of this book.

In addition to the "Limbo of the Lost," several other areas exist throughout the world where an unusually large number of unexplainable sea mysteries happen. The most famous is a region located southeast of Japan in the Pacific Ocean. Ships and boats have been disappearing in that area for more than a century, and in the early 1950s almost a dozen large ships vanished without leaving a trace to tell their tragic tales.

Since 1955, seamen have been avoiding this region. Scientists have stated that the previous mishaps theoretically could have been caused by volcanic explosions catching ships unexpectedly in their eruptions. While this theory is plausible, the question that is constantly being asked, not only of the Pacific area but also of the "Limbo of the Lost," is: "Why no debris, survivors, bodies, lifeboats, or oil slicks?"

The major difference between other mysterious sea regions of the world and the "Limbo" zone is that not only are ships engulfed but aircraft as well disappear far beyond the laws of chance.

# II

# Plane Disappearances
# in the "Limbo of the Lost"

# Summary of Major Plane Disappearances Within the "Limbo of the Lost"

| | |
|---|---|
| July 18, 1945 | PB-4YW, with 15 crew members. |
| Dec. 5, 1945 | 5 TBM-3 Avengers and 1 Martin Mariner PBM Flying Boat, with a total of 27 crew members for the 6 planes. |
| July 3, 1947 | C-54, with 6 crew members. |
| Jan. 30, 1948 | *Star Tiger*, a British South American Airways passenger plane, with 31 passengers and crew. |
| Dec. 28, 1948 | DC-3A passenger plane, with 30 passengers and crew. |
| Jan. 17, 1949 | *Star Ariel*, a sister ship of the *Star Tiger*, a British South American passenger plane, with 19 passengers and crew. |
| Oct. 30, 1954 | Navy 4-engine Super-Constellation, with 42 passengers and crew. |
| Nov. 9, 1956 | Navy Martin Marlin P5M twin-engine patrol flying boat, with crew of 10. |
| Jan. 8, 1962 | KB-50J refueling tanker, with crew of 9. |
| Sept. 22, 1963 | C-133 Cargomaster, with crew of 10. |

# The Lost Training Mission, Wednesday, December 5, 1945

Planes missing: 5 TBM-3 Avenger torpedo bombers
1 Martin Mariner PBM Flying Boat

Personnel missing: 27

Getting ready for takeoff from the runway of Fort Lauderdale, U.S. Air Naval Station, were five Navy Grumman, TBM-3 Avenger torpedo bombers.

The World War II sea-combat-designed aircraft normally carried a crew of three. However, one crewman scheduled for the mission was unable to report for duty on that ill-fated day.

Each pilot went through his own preflight check:

Fuel—maximum 18,250 pounds (enough for over 1,000 miles).

Instruments and compass—check.

Radio—checked with tower and command pilot.

Lifesaving equipment—Mae West and self-inflating life raft—check.

At two o'clock, right on schedule, the five TBM's took off, assumed flight formation, and headed out to sea toward the Bahamas. Several routine position reports were received, but then at 5:25 P.M. (EST) a distress message from the mission's flight leader puzzled control tower officials:

"We seem to be lost . . . Have enough fuel for 75 more minutes . . . Can't tell whether over Atlantic or Gulf . . . Not sure, but think we are 75 miles northeast of the Banana River Naval Air Station" (located about

10

200 miles northeast of Miami). These were the last words received.

From the tempo of the conversation, the control tower personnel at Fort Lauderdale got the impression that the flight was caught in a blinding storm, but why couldn't they resume radio contact with any of the five planes?

As the last report was received from the TBM's, Commander Howard S. Roberts, executive officer of the station, was in the tower. He immediately signaled air-sea rescue, and within minutes a huge Martin Mariner (PBM) flying boat lumbered into the air, fully equipped for rescue duty with a trained crew of 13.

According to officials, there was nothing to be overly concerned about because Avengers were known to have a high degree of buoyancy. "When other TBM's were downed at sea, the crews were able to launch their life rafts without even getting their feet wet."

Fort Lauderdale kept in constant contact with the rescue PBM. At approximately 7:30 P.M., the tower reported it was unable to raise the flying boat by radio.

Throughout the night, the Coast Guard patrolled the seas while Navy planes scoured an area 275 miles northeast of Miami.

Navy officials reported that the baby flattop, U.S.S. *Solomons,* an escort aircraft carrier located off the southwest Florida coast, had launched her 30 fighter planes into the search. Every plane available from the British Royal Air Force base at Wind Wor Field in the Bahamas was in the sky. Third Air Force stationed at Tampa was aloft, and the Air Transport Command from Miami joined in flying low over the Everglades and the flat Florida land. All available patrol and merchant vessels in Florida waters had also joined in the hunt. In all, 252 Navy planes, hundreds of Army and Coast Guard planes and a fleet of surface craft were 150 miles out in the Atlantic, from north of Jacksonville to the Bahamas.

Naval officials admitted they had nothing new to report Thursday morning, but they added that hope had not yet been abandoned. The great search armada was joined by a large "Dumbo" flying boat, equipped with a detachable lifeboat. The destroyer tender *Shenandoah* and the Coast Guard cutter *Pandora* moved into the extended area 350 miles out on a line reaching from Palm Beach to St. Augustine. All at once, as if a tap was turned on, a flurry of conflicting reports was received from the search task force.

Meanwhile, the merchant ship *Gaines Mills,* had reported that its crew had seen an explosion in the air and what appeared to be an airplane spin down into the ocean at approximately 7:50 Wednesday night. The vessel's captain was unable to give the exact location, but at the time of the reported incident the *Gaines Mills* was off the coast of New Smyrna Beach, Florida.

Dozens of planes and surface craft were dispatched to the reported area, but no wreckage, oil, or other clues were found. The aerial hunt was then farther extended 200 miles out to sea in a 400-mile front down the Florida coast, from Jacksonville in the north to Miami in the south.

The three-day-old hunt for the lost fliers was suddenly intensified when an Eastern Airlines pilot, Captain J. D. Morrison, reported to the Navy that he saw red flares and flashing lights "in the middle of a swamp" at about two o'clock Saturday morning, ten miles southwest of Melbourne, Florida. Captain Morrison, piloting a northbound passenger plane, was quoted as saying he saw human figures standing in the light of the flares but could not discern any wreckage. "I'm sure they were flares, not a fire," he said.

Five minutes after his first communiqué, Captain Morrison reported he saw a fire burning in the dismal, sparsely populated region some 20 miles north of the spot where he had seen the flares.

A Navy plane was dispatched from the Banana River Naval Air Station. At 2:30 A.M., the pilot radioed that he also observed a flare about 50 miles inland.

At dawn, a dense fog limited the visibility of aerial searchers to almost zero. The main hope of a rescue was centered on a small land army of wartime assault craft, weasels, marsh buggies, alligators, and jeeps that groped their way through the bleak swamplands of north central Florida. Throughout the day, shuttling sweeps of Army, Navy, and Coast Guard planes, plus a Navy blimp from Lakehurst, New Jersey, flew over the wild, desolate region. A helicopter also made a number of landings and sent men out to comb the marsh on foot in an attempt to locate wreckage or survivors.

Commander H. H. J. Benson of the U.S. 7th Naval District said, "We don't want to get any hopes too high, but I would like to report that we are moving everything up there to find those men if they are alive." He went on to say that the hunt was being pressed with all available forces and disclosed that farmers in the Melbourne-Orlando area reported hearing an explosion on the night the six planes vanished. Commander Benson was quoted as saying, "This is the first time a whole flight of planes ever disappeared without a trace."

A pilot of an Army Air Corps plane reported seeing two men aboard two life rafts. He stated that the men waved as he flew toward their rafts, but when he made his run over their crafts he could no longer see the men.

A Naval spokesman cast doubt on the report by saying that two survivors, no matter how exhausted, would never collapse simultaneously with rescue so near at hand after seeing a plane. The Navy's position was supported when the alleged rafts were found to be nothing more than packing cases bobbing in the waters some 300 miles due east of Melbourne.

Hope was raised again when a report was received stating that two survivors had been rescued at sea by the tanker *Erwin Russell*. This too turned out to be erroneous. The Navy said the tanker's original report in effect read, "Lowering lifeboats to pick up survivors from raft." Subsequently, the tanker radioed air-sea rescue headquarters in Miami stating that they had made a mistake; instead of survivors or life raft, it had only found a tow-target used by the Navy for gunnery practice at sea.

A further report was received from the Army airfield at Boca Raton saying that the pilot, copilot, and 9 crewmen of an Army B-24 had found 2 life rafts close together in an area 290 miles east of Melbourne. They were almost sure they had seen two men huddled in one of the rafts.

The pilot, Leonard Bostick, and his copilot Eugene B. Hollander, were quoted as saying they flew over the rafts for about four and a half hours before a failing gas supply compelled them to return to base. An extract from their official report reads as follows: "At 10:45 A.M. [EST] we located rafts and circled over them. While circling we saw two one-man rafts apparently tied together. At the beginning every man in the crew believed there were two men in the rafts. However, as the day wore on we could not be sure." Bostick related how they flew down to an altitude of several hundred feet, but heavy winds prevented them from going lower for closer observation. He said they tried to direct surface vessels to the rafts but no contacts were made by the time they were forced to leave the scene.

An extensive air-sea search was conducted in and around the reported area but again without success.

The Coast Guard cutter the *Vigilante* reported sighting "something which could have been a parachute," 180 miles east of Melbourne. Later the cutter radioed that it had scoured the particular area without locating anything that might be remotely considered a clue.

As hope for rescue faded, only 66 planes took to the skies at dawn on December 10. Most of the aircraft, a number of merchant ships, and one destroyer-tender had been released from further search operations.

Naval officials announced that the air-sea rescue operation would be called off at dusk unless new evidence could be discovered. They expressed fear of ever finding any of the fliers alive, but added, "We have not given up yet; if those men are still alive we'll do everything to find them."

Search craft carried out orders of the last day of the quest by combing 25,000 square miles, yard by yard, for even a slight clue. As darkness blacked out the sea, the Navy disclosed that 930 air sorties and many searches by 30 ships were made in the futile 5-day hunt. Every possibility had been explored before the search was discontinued. Three hundred eighty thousand square miles of sea, coast, land, and swamps were combed without uncovering a single shred of evidence that any of the 27 fliers were still alive. Navy officials stressed that planes and surface craft which travel the area where the airmen are believed to have disappeared would remain on the alert indefinitely.

Within informed circles, numerous theories regarding the unusual disappearance were advanced and discussed. These fell into several categories:

*1. All six planes experienced engine trouble*

The possibility that all six planes experienced engine trouble and crashed without leaving a trace is too farfetched to bear any weight.

*2. A mass air collision or a freak water spout which plucked planes out of sky*

These theories would account for the abrupt interruption of radio contact. Certainly a tremendous amount of debris, a gigantic oil slick, and several bodies would have remained to tell the tale. What about the Martin Mariner flying boat—could it have met the same fate?

*3. Magnetic disturbance affecting all compasses, causing planes to fly in circles until fuel was exhausted*

According to Coast Guard officials, no reports were ever filed pertaining to magnetic disturbances in the area of the "Limbo of the Lost." If the planes ran into a magnetic storm that affected their compasses, they would not fly in circles but would have set a bearing on the sun setting above the western horizon. If the planes ran out of fuel for one reason or another, all of the crew were trained in ditching procedures and could exist for many days in the open sea.

*4. Unknown type of atmospheric aberration swallowed all the planes*

Officially, the Navy said the theory of a "hole in the sky" did not exist, nor had one existed in the past.

*5. Adverse weather conditions*

The U.S. Weather Bureau in Miami reported freak winds, attended by gusts of 40 miles per hour or higher, as well as showers and thunderstorms prevailing over the area off the Banana River Station at the time when the last message was received from the Avengers.

A Navy spokesman explained that the gusts were not strong enough to blow the TBM's off their course.

After a lengthy and most detailed investigation, the Department of the Navy issued a statement affirming that the combat-training flight leader in charge of the Avenger's group and all of the crew members involved in the flight were experienced from slightly over one to over six years. The statement discounted the possibility that the planes might have developed flight trouble and landed at other fields, pointing out that if that had happened their home base would have been notified immediately.

The Naval Board of Inquiry concluded its investigation without the advantage of having a trace of real evidence to work with. They listened to testimony of witnesses and studied the few facts available. The board expressed complete bafflement that all six planes could simply disappear without leaving a trace or clue. A board officer was quoted as saying, "This unprecedented peacetime loss seems to be a total mystery, the strangest ever investigated in the annals of Naval aviation." To this day, no logical solution to the disappearances has ever been found.

At a press conference called on the morning of the fourth anniversary of the bombing of Pearl Harbor, the names of the missing fliers were released.

A typical example of the caliber and experience of the downed fliers was Marine Sergeant Robert Francis Gallivan, 21, of Northampton, Massachusetts. Gallivan had been in the Marines for four years. He took his basic training at Paris Island, South Carolina, early in 1942 and then transferred to the Marine Air Force. He was sent to the South Pacific where he served 18 months winning a Commendation Ribbon in addition to the American and Pacific Theater Ribbons. Gallivan returned to the United States in November 1945 and, after a 30-day leave at home, reported to Cherry Point, North Carolina, then to Fort Lauderdale Naval Air Station, Florida.

Recently the author talked to Mrs. Gallivan about the disappearance of her son. She stated that on December 6, 1945, she didn't go to work because it was the day Robert was to be home from the service for good.

Instead of her son, a telegram arrived from the War Department stating that he was missing at sea. Mrs. Gallivan sadly commented, when it was all over, that Navy officials only remarked that the disappearance of Robert Francis Gallivan was just one of those strange unsolved mysteries of the sea.

Other personnel among the 14 officers and enlisted men on the patrol bombers included:

Arm. 3/c Walter Reed Parpart, Jr.—Brooklyn, N.Y.
Arm. 3/c George F. Beulin—Brooklyn, N.Y.

Seaman 3/c Bert Edward Valuk, Jr.—Bloomfield, N.J.
Pfc. Robert Peter Gruebbl, USMC—Maspeth, N.Y.
Capt. Edward Joseph Powers, Jr., USMC—Vernon, N.Y.
S/Sgt. George Richard Paonessa, USMC—Mamaroneck, N.Y.

Among the men on the missing Navy (PBM) search plane was:

Seaman 1/c P. S. Neeman—North Hill, Pa.

## The Lost PB-4YW, Wednesday, July 18, 1945
### Personnel missing: 15

Less than five months before the five TBM patrol planes disappeared, another Navy plane had vanished. Every air-sea rescue unit in south Florida and the Royal Air Force from the Bahamas had been mobilized to hunt for a missing PB-4YW, 4-engine, Privateer with 4 officers and 11 enlisted men on board.

Lieutenant William C. Bailey of New York piloted the big plane off the runway of Miami Naval Air Station on a routine training mission. The single-tailed version of the Army's B-24 headed out to sea at 12:26, Wednesday morning, July 18, 1945, and never returned.

A gigantic but futile air-sea search was conducted without turning up anything, either in the sea or on the beaches. It was as though a small dress rehearsal had been conducted by whatever lurks in the "Limbo of the Lost."

19

# The Missing C-54
## Thursday, July 3, 1947

### Personnel missing: 6

Americans everywhere were finalizing plans for Independence Day celebrations, when word was flashed to the Coast Guard, Army Air Corps, and Navy stationed along the lower eastern seaboard that a four-engine, Army C-54 cargo transport plane with its crew of six was missing at sea. The report stated that the overdue aircraft took off Thursday morning, July 3, 1947, from Kindley Field, Bermuda, for Morrison Army Air Field, Palm Beach, Florida. Estimated time of arrival was scheduled for mid-afternoon.

Ships and planes raced out to play their role in the by now all-too-familiar search pattern extending from the coast of Florida to Bermuda. Hunters scanned the seas all night for a glimpse of light. By dawn, the air-sea rescue operation was in full swing, with hopes high of finding the fliers alive.

Early Friday morning, July 4, a large Army transport C-74 reported sighting wreckage on the sea 300 miles northeast of West Palm Beach, Florida. Army authorities said the Navy cargo ship *Orion* was plowing toward the area to determine if the debris was that of the missing plane. The C-74 was acting as guide for the surface craft when poor visibility and communication difficulties hampered and slowed the rescue efforts.

For hours, the press awaited word from the *Orion*.

Finally, Major L. R. Humphreys, commanding the 5th Air Rescue Squadron at Morrison Field released details of the find. He reported that the cargo ship found an oxygen bottle, two yellow seat cushions, and some aircraft plywood—all believed to be Army aircraft equipment, but none of it identified as belonging to the lost plane.

Air Transport Command (ATC) headquarters announced that the search for the C-54 and its crew was officially abandoned as of Tuesday, July 8, 1947. According to the statement, the only wreckage found in the course of the 110,000-square-mile search by Army, Navy, and Coast Guard planes and surface vessels was that picked up by the *Orion*. No other debris, bodies, oil slick, or clues turned up. The ATC alone flew 52 sorties involving 422 hours of flight.

All planes and ships in the vicinity of the search route were asked to continue the hunt, if at all possible. But to this day, the mystery of what happened to the Army C-54 and crew of six remains the secret of the "Limbo of the Lost."

In a later official statement, the commanding officer of Kindley Field, Bermuda, released the names of the following men, all members of his command:

Maj. Ralph B. Ward, Pilot and operations director of Kindley Field—Concord, N.H.
Maj. Clyde R. Inman, Copilot—Boise, Idaho
Maj. John R. Sands, Jr., Navigator—Jacksonville, Fla.
S/Sgt. Andrew S. Bagacus, Aerial Engineer—Townsend, Wis.
Sgt. Fred E. Fricks, Assistant Aerial Engineer—Chattanooga, Tenn.
S/Sgt. Ernest D. Fey, Radio Operator—New Orleans, La.

The wives of all these men were living in Bermuda at the time of the plane's disappearance, as well as the son of Major Inman and the son and daughter of Sergeant Fricks.

# A Passenger Plane Vanishes!

## The Mysterious Disappearance of the *Star Tiger*, Friday, January 30, 1948

### Passengers and crew missing: 31

As the world received word that Orville Wright, co-inventor of the airplane died, one of the greatest peacetime air-sea searches ever conducted was being carried out in the Atlantic northeast of Bermuda. A desperate attempt was underway to find 25 passengers and 6 crewmen reported missing along with their British South American Airways, 4-engine, Avro, Tudor IV, luxury airliner, *Star Tiger*.

The 32-passenger plane, on a flight from London to Havana, was on its third stage from Santa Maria in the Azores to Hamilton, Bermuda, a distance of 1,960 miles.

A radio message sent by the *Star Tiger*'s pilot, Captain David Colby, at 10:30 Thursday night, January 29, established that he would reach Hamilton at approximately 1:00 A.M. (EST), an hour and a half late.

At about 1:00 A.M. Captain Colby radioed, "Still approximately 440 miles northeast of Bermuda and

22

bucking strong headwinds." That was the last message heard from the *Star Tiger*.

When the Tudor IV was reported overdue, Hamilton tower tried to establish radio contact without success. Air-sea rescue headquarters was alerted. It was estimated the Avro had enough fuel to last until approximately 3:15 A.M.

If the *Star Tiger* had been forced down, the chances were that it could have floated long enough for successful survival operations.

Captain Leslie S. Cruthirds at search headquarters stated that the main hope of the rescue units was that the *Star Tiger*'s pilot was able to ditch the huge plane without seriously damaging the fuselage. The Tudor IV, similar to the U.S. Air Force C-54, is sufficiently pressurized and hermetically sealed that, if undamaged, there would be time to allow everyone aboard to get set free in the rubber life rafts she carried.

The temperature of the water in the search area was about 65 degrees, meaning that there was a good chance for those who managed to get aboard a raft. Each life raft was equipped with a survival kit which included a "Gibson Girl," a small hand-cranked radio designed to be held between the knees. It operated on the 500 kilocycles band, and the range was generally limited to a radius of 50 to a few hundred miles, depending upon the kind of antenna used.

Direction of the search operations was assigned to Colonel Thomas D. Ferguson, commander of the United States Air Force Base in Bermuda.

Two USAF Flying Fortresses from Bermuda's Kindley Field and another from MacDill Field, Florida, were the first search craft underway. The B-17's carried the latest lifeboats, designed to be dropped by parachute. Also 2 B-25 bombers and a C-47 transport from Mitchell Field, New York, were assigned the area from Ocean City, New Jersey, north to Long Island, and eastward out over the Atlantic for 500 miles. All aircraft were equipped with several life rafts. Six other planes at Mitchell Field were placed on standby alert.

The Coast Guard aired three PBY amphibian airplanes plus three cutters, the *Mendota* from Wilmington, North Carolina, the *Cherokee* from Norfolk, Virginia, and the *Androscoggin* from New York. The cutters were dispatched by Eastern Area Search and Rescue Headquarters of the Coast Guard in New York.

Two commercial steamers and a British South American Airways plane were sent out to work over a large area 300 to 400 miles northeast and east of Bermuda.

The Air Transport Command (ATC) announced that 14 of its planes had joined the search. A spokesman for ATC in Washington, D.C., said the planes would continue the hunt and that others would be added if the *Star Tiger* was not found in the meantime. A C-54 transport of ATC, bound from the Azores to the United States, and a B-17 Flying Fortress, in which Major General William E. Hall was flying to Germany, were pressed into the hunt when they landed at Bermuda.

Six 4-engine transports of Pan American World Airways flying the New York to San Juan, Puerto Rico, route were ordered to leave their usual course and swing over the area in which it was believed the Tudor IV was lost. However, rain squalls and limited visibility made searching difficult.

Search planes became airborne from bases as far

north as Stephensville, Newfoundland, to as far south as Borninquen Air Force Base, San Juan. Planes were dispatched or alerted from every base along the Atlantic coast.

The Coast Guard had 3 speedy sea-going motor launches, 30, 60, and 105 feet long, at Hamilton on standby with orders to put to sea at once if life rafts were located.

Desk officers and ground crews at Kindley Field volunteered to go aloft in B-29's attached to the Weather Reconnaissance Squadron and in other planes as observers, so that all flight trained officers and enlisted men could be assigned to flight operations duties.

As the sun went down on the first day of the big hunt, Colonel Ferguson at search command headquarters reported that all his planes had been grounded because of adverse weather conditions. The hunt would continue at dawn unless adverse weather conditions again balked their efforts.

One of the search pilots said, "I doubt anyone could survive in seas like that." Other search pilots reported that the weather was stormy, with waves up to 40 feet high.

Several clues, possibly connected with the *Star Tiger*, were reported from different areas.

Part of the search fleet was diverted, for a time, to a position northwest of Bermuda, when Captain W. R. Richards, eastern area chief of staff of the Coast Guard received a report sent by the 5,800-ton, S. S. *Troubador*.

The message said, "Sighted low-flying plane with lights blinking at 2:10 A.M. [EST] halfway between Bermuda and the Delaware Bay entrance." Captain

Richards said it was possible the plane could have overshot Bermuda because of a squall that hit the island at about the time the plane was due there.

Later it was learned that the reported craft was a Pan American World Airways plane and definitely not in trouble.

As a result of a report sent by the pilot of a B-17 out of Westover Field, Massachusetts, the Coast Guard sent surface cutters to an area between Bermuda and Cape Hatteras, North Carolina. The pilot said he spotted what was believed to be a cylindrical object, plus yellow and black boxes floating nearby.

When the cutters, *Cherokee,* and *Androscoggin* and the Coast Guard tug *Acushnet,* reached the area, they reported finding only a roll of sheet cork which from the air could look like a cylinder, but no sign of the other reported objects—only rough seas, lowering skies, and winds of near gale force.

Captain W. M. Hackett, pilot of a search plane, reported oil slicks 240 miles northwest of Bermuda.

Another pilot reported sighting oil patches 500 miles east-northeast of Bermuda.

Still another pilot reported spotting an oil slick between 75 and 100 miles northeast of Bermuda.

A search of all reported areas showed no trace of the missing plane. Search and Rescue Headquarters of the Coast Guard in New York pointed out that the slicks described most probably were caused by bilge pumping from passing steamers.

Two Pan American planes reported flares and a raft to the south of Bermuda.

The flares were never confirmed, but the tanker *Esso Philadelphia,* called to the scene, reported that the raft found was launched from a surface vessel, and it had been in the water a long time.

On Monday, February 2, G. S. Lindgren, parliamentary secretary of the British Ministry of Civil Aviation, announced to the House of Commons that a public inquiry would be made into the loss of the Tudor IV airliner *Star Tiger*. He said the ministry would seek technical advice from the Air Registration Board and that all Tudor IV's had been withdrawn from service.

A spokesman for the British South American Airways Corporation said his company knew no reason why the Air Registration Board should not assure the Ministry of Civil Aviation of the airworthiness of the Tudor IV. As soon as this assurance had been received, use of the aircraft would certainly be resumed.

The airline had been operating three Tudor IV's on the Bermuda route, the first of which came into service in October 1947.

Officials of the British Overseas Airways Corporation (BOAC), which also used Tudor IV's, said the grounding would not affect the company's overall operation.

All available planes at Bermuda were ordered to continue the search. Forty aircraft flew over 200,000 square miles of ocean on overlapping courses. Although the air and surface hunt was being continued, hope was fading rapidly, and it was feared that all aboard the *Star Tiger* were lost.

Hope for survivors was revived as amateur and professional radio operators from Halifax to Miami reported picking up several radio messages in code that spelled out the name "Tiger." Others reported hearing "Star Tiger" spelled out. The code messages were picked up on an international channel for voice communication in an emergency; however, voice was not used.

Navy and Canadian Air Force officers in Halifax reported that the signals were of an improvised code nature, in which someone laboriously tapped out one dot for "A," two dots for "B," and so on, through the alphabet.

The signals were heard late Tuesday night, February 3 and were not picked up during the day. All Navy, Coast Guard, aviation, and shipping radios from Canada to South America listened for the signals to resume.

The Federal Communications Commission sent out sensitive, mobile direction-finding units in an effort to pick up the signals and triangulate their position. If such a fix can be made from three points, the location of the sender can be approximated.

Search officials emphatically denied that the downed plane could have survived this long in the water or that any of the *Star Tiger*'s heavy radio gear could possibly have been put on a raft. If anybody was still alive, why didn't he use the light "Gibson Girl" transmitter provided for just such an emergency?

In any event 40 aircraft at Kindley Field and various other fields along the southern coast were standing by. Coast Guard cutters remained waiting in the areas where wreckage and oil slicks were reported.

No further signals were heard. The only logical explanation was that some person, or persons, with a twisted mind sent the messages as a prank.

The British Ministry of Civil Aviation announced in London that it was "presumed" the plane and its passengers and crew had been lost at sea.

On September 28, 1948, the verdict of the court

appointed by the Minister of Civil Aviation to investigate the disappearance of the *Star Tiger* was published as a White Paper (Cmd. 7517, Stationery Office, 2s.).

The fate of the *Star Tiger*, the British South American Airways liner, must remain an unsolved mystery. "It may truly be said that no more baffling problem has ever been presented for investigation."

There were no grounds to suppose that the design of the Tudor IV aircraft caused the mishap. No evidence existed leading to possible technical errors or omissions. The possiblities that fire broke out, a disastrous mechanical breakdown took place, or any part of the plane's power plant caused the disappearance is remote and most improbable.

The final paragraph of the report reads: "In the complete absence of any reliable evidence as to either the nature or the cause of the disaster to the *Star Tiger*, the court has not been able to do more than suggest possibilities, none of which reaches the level even of probability. What happened in this case will never be known."

Losses of passengers and crew on the *Star Tiger* included the following persons:

*Eighteen British:*
Air Marshal Sir Arthur Coningham, Royal Air Force, who Commanded the 2d Tactical Air Force of the Allies at the invasion of Normandy and was considered one of the world's foremost authorities on the use of tactical air power in cooperation with ground armies. Sir Arthur was on his way to Nassau and planned to spend a few days in Bermuda with Sir Richard Fairey, head of a British aircraft manufacturing company that bears his name.
Assistant Secretary of the British Treasury, H. Ernest Brooks. Mr. Brooks was bound for Bermuda on business.
Major and Mrs. A. T. Barwell—Argyll, Scotland

Thomas Walton Davies—Kelvedon, Essex, Eng.

Eric Fisher—Totteridge, North London, Eng.

Cyril Morton Hawley—Windsor, Bershire, Eng.

Mr. and Mrs. Anthony John Mulligan and Thomas R. J. Mulligan—London, Eng.

Mrs. Sylvia Nebel, Miss Edith Nebel, and Manfred and Vilem Nebel—Langley, Eng.

George Keith Riddock—London, Eng.

Robert Charles Staley—Wallsend, Northumberland, Eng.

Mrs. Georgina Strong—Dunfermline, Scotland

John Matthews Sutherland—Leigh-on-Sea, Eng.

*Two Czechoslovakians:*
Elias Klein and his wife who gave an address in Havana, Cuba

*One Swiss:*
Harold Gordon Cabrett—Zurich, Switzerland

*Two Mexicans:*
One name unknown.
Mr. Ignacio Echegaray Jauregul mailed a letter to his wife from Santa Maria airport. He told of having to wait there 19 hours and added: "The weather is still bad. We don't know whether we will leave within an hour, or tomorrow or the next day, via New York. When we came here we were being blown by a 100-kilometer-an-hour wind and we were about to be blown to Canada or down into the ocean."

# The Loss of The Holiday DC-3A Excursion Passenger Plane

## Tuesday, December 28, 1948

### Passengers and crew missing: 30

Twenty-seven passengers, including two babies, boarded a chartered twin-engine DC-3A airliner at San Juan Airport. Most of the passengers were Puerto

Ricans returning to New York from a holiday excursion visit to their homeland for Christmas.

The pilot, Captain Robert Linquist of Ft. Myers, Florida, filed his instrument flight plan, designating departure San Juan—destination New York, with a stopover scheduled for Miami, estimated time of arrival 4:30 A.M. (EST).

The copilot, Ernie E. Hill, Jr., 22, of Miami, completed the preflight check as the stewardess, Mary Burke of Jersey City, New Jersey, checked off the passenger list.

At 10:30 P.M., December 27, with everything in order for the long 1,200-mile flight, the big plane, loaded to capacity, took off into the dark clear skies of the West Indies.

A position report was received by the Airways Radio Station at Kingston, Jamaica, shortly after 1:00 A.M.

At 4:13 A.M. the Civil Aeronautics Overseas Radio at New Orleans, Louisiana, picked up a faint position report in which Captain Linquist stated his position as "50 miles south of Miami."

This would place the DC-3 well within sight of land. The Overseas Radio repeated the position to the plane and asked confirmation.

There was no answer. Repeated calls brought no response. An alert was sounded and other stations attempted to reach the aircraft by radio, without results.

The DC-3 was owned by Karl Knight of Miami, but had been leased to Airborne Transport, Inc. of New York. Mr. Knight said he had nothing to do with the operation of the leased craft. He learned it was missing when, landing another plane, he heard Airways Radio making urgent requests to the silent charter flight to respond to messages.

Air-sea rescue was alerted for fear the big plane had crashed in the area of the Florida Keys, and an immediate air and surface hunt was launched. The coastal waters in the region of the Keys is so clear and shallow that the DC-3, if there, could easily have been seen on the bottom.

At dawn, when search craft reported finding nothing in the vicinity of the Keys, a fleet of 43 airplanes of the Army, Navy, and Coast Guard from Florida and the Caribbean began the far-flung patrol spreading over the Florida straits, northern Cuba, the Bahama Islands, and the air route from Miami to San Juan. The search was later extended to the entire Florida peninsula, Charleston, South Carolina, the east end of Cuba, and the eastern Gulf of Mexico. At nightfall a Navy blimp joined the hunt.

A Coast Guard officer said the DC-3's fuel would have been used up by about 5:45 A.M. He pointed out that the plane was fully equipped with survival gear including a "Gibson Girl" emergency radio, life rafts, and individual life preservers.

Gusty weather hampered the widespread search somewhat, but Coast Guard officials said there were few cancellations among the vast fleet of aircraft and ships combing the seas.

Several survival reports later proved to be without foundation.

A report was received by a ship that it had sighted flares in the area of the Bahamas.

Seven Air Force planes were dispatched into the region and a thorough search was conducted, but, as before, the results were negative.

Two air-sea rescue planes spotted the remains of a badly burned plane on Andros Island in the Bahamas.

A land party was flown to the scene. The mystery of the missing DC-3 continued when the land group reported the wreckage was that of an old wartime plane known to have crashed many years before.

An unconfirmed report was received at the Coast Guard's air-sea rescue headquarters that survivors were sighted on a beach in Cuba. A spokesman said, "The information did not even designate on which side of the island the survivors were believed sighted, but we plan to scour every inch of coastline, if necessary, in the hope that we may sight something." He emphasized that the report was entirely unofficial. If nothing was found on the east end of Cuba, the Coast Guard official said, they would extend the search to the south side of Cuba.

Military aircraft in the vicinity were diverted to Cuba's coastline on the offchance that the rumor was correct. A complete sweep proved the lead unfounded.

At dusk, Monday, January 10, the Coast Guard announced that all clues leading to the whereabouts of the DC-3 charter flight had been exhausted.

Several hundred thousand square miles of sea, coast, and land had been scanned from the Caribbean and Gulf to the Keys and Everglades, without turning up debris, bodies, or even an oil slick.

Not so much as a trace remained to tell the fate of the 30 persons who flew into the unknown moments of the "Limbo of the Lost."

The official passenger list for the missing DC-3 charter plane and destination of the passengers were listed as follows:

*New York:*
Hilda Rivera, 23, 55 West 48th St.
Ramón Alvarez, 21, 55 West 48th St.
Emilia Pérez, 22, 112 East 96th St.
Edmundo Carriga, 21, 319 West 48th St.
Jacinto Mercado, 22, 319 West 48th St.
Juan Ortiz, 24, 319 West 48th St.
Francisco Sánchez, 29, 319 West 48th St.
Jose Sanabria, 20, 1744 Lexington Ave.
Maria Ayala, 27, 1744 Lexington Ave.
Irene Rivera, 27, 1744 Lexington Ave.
Juan Rivera Ortega, 28, 244 East 117th St.
Francisco Delgado, 34, 244 East 117th St.
Esther Santiago, 26, 108 East 111th St.
Félix Rodríguez, 28, 319 West 48th St.
Leoncio Perez, 55 West 48th St.

*Miami:*

| | |
|---|---|
| Pedro Carrasquilla, 32 | Antonio Muñoz, 24 |
| Cenare Figueroa, 20 | Vidal Rodríguez, 30 |
| Juan M. Pérez, 23 | Ramón Rodríguez, 30 |
| Carmen Vázquez, 22 | Carmela Valesquez, 28 |

*Lorain, Ohio:*

| | |
|---|---|
| Florencio Rivera, 38 | Juan Rodríguez, 30 |

Two babies were also aboard.


# The Disappearance of Another British South American Airways Passenger Plane, Monday, January 17, 1949

## Passengers and crew missing: 18

Catastrophe once again struck the British South American Airways Corporation just 13 days short of a year since the disappearance of their airliner *Star Tiger*. This time it was her sister aircraft *Star Ariel* that vanished.

The four-engine Tudor IV passenger plane departed Bermuda on a 6-hour, 1,000-mile flight to Kingston, Jamaica, at 7:42 A.M. (EST), Monday, January 17, 1949. It was the second leg of her flight from London Airport to Santiago, Chile, estimated time of arrival scheduled for 1:42 P.M.

Captain J. C. McPhee, the *Ariel*'s pilot, radioed Bermuda Radio Control at 8:50 A.M. that he was changing frequency to make contact with Jamaica Control. By 10:10 A.M., BSAA officials at Jamaica had tried to establish contact with the big passenger plane without success. Two hours and 28 minutes after the last radio report was received, an air-sea rescue alert was sounded.

Bermuda authorities said that Captain McPhee's plane had enough gasoline for ten hours of flying. Although the *Ariel* was carrying only 12 passengers and a crew of 6, she had a seating capacity of 32. Her full designation was Avro, Tudor IV, Post War, pressurized cabin Luxury Airliner. The Tudor IV had five emergency exits, carried three large dinghies, one fitted with a radio transmitter, and life belts were stowed under the passenger seats and in the crew's compartment.

With the *Star Airel*'s fuel tanks evidently drained at 5:42 P.M. and the plane still missing, the Coast Guard marshaled its forces and formed plans for an extensive search to begin at dawn. Meanwhile, just before dusk, a U.S. Army plane from Kindley Field, Bermuda, made a sweep of the area of the Tudor's last reported position, without sighting anything. All ships and aircraft along the big plane's route and in the area of the western

Caribbean were alerted by radio to keep a sharp lookout.

MacDill Field said a B-29 Superfortress was scheduled to take off at 3:00 A.M. and a B-17 at 5:00 A.M. The Coast Guard in New York relayed the message that rescue planes from Salem, Massachusetts, Brooklyn, New York, and Elizabeth City, North Carolina, would go to Bermuda and begin intensive flights over the search area at daybreak. Other planes from Florida Coast Guard bases and planes of the other services were alerted. Nassau reported aircraft would leave at dawn to search the eastern Bahamas. A U.S. Navy plane equipped with radar was set to go aloft from the Guantanamo base in Cuba. Aircraft carriers *Kearsarge* and *Leyte* and the battleship *Missouri* joined six U.S. destroyers thrown into the search from Jamaica.

As the sun broke through the darkness, planes and ships began the tremendous task of looking for the proverbial "drop in the ocean." By high noon the Coast Guard announced that an estimated 72 search planes, many ships, and approximately 13,000 men were actively engaged in the hunt for life.

As the days passed without finding a trace of the *Star Ariel,* the U.S. Air Force added 16 more planes, 12 B-29's, 2 Catalina flying boats, and 2 B-17's from the United States, with orders assigning them to Hamilton, Bermuda.

Pan American World Airways instructed pilots of two of its planes en route from San Juan to Miami to change course and search the area. BSAA, operators of the *Ariel* ordered another Tudor IV, which left Nassau, Bahama, to make the hunt. The entire personnel of the Cuban Armed Services were placed on search alert.

Bermuda reported that planes flying in relays had

scoured over 150,000 square miles of ocean in an area roughly 125 to 500 miles to the south-southwest, without finding any survivors, a trace of wreckage, or even an oil slick. Spokesmen stressed the fact that not a single message denoting trouble of any kind had been received from the *Ariel* after she asked Bermuda Radio Control to transfer her to Jamaica Control about an hour after departure from Hamilton. As in the loss of the *Tiger,* searchers also were mystified by the lack of any SOS distress message.

A British South American Airways Constellation pilot reported early in the morning of January 20 that he twice sighted lights on the water and then what his crew thought was a floating object reflected in the light of the moon.

The crew said the light was seen 300 miles southsouthwest of Bermuda. An Air Force spokesman added that search craft had been out flying wing tip to wing tip, over the reported area, in both an upper and lower covering, but had not sighted anything. Search headquarters issued a statement that they held out little hope of developments.

Interest in the search increased during the afternoon of January 22, when one of the hunt planes spotted a yellow object measuring five feet by four feet, presumably the same object previously reported.

Aerial investigation proved the reported sighting to be a large box that could not possibly be connected with the lost aircraft.

The possibility that sabotage was responsible for the disappearance was raised in London by Sir Roy Dobson, managing director of A. V. Roe & Co., Ltd., makers of Tudor planes. This explanation was dismissed because most certainly a tremendous amount of debris would have been found.

Lord Pakenham, Minister of Civil Aviation, announced in the House of Lords that BSAA had temporarily grounded its Tudor IV's for a special examination.

The Tudor-type aircraft had been the subject of considerable controversy in British parliamentary and aviation circles since it went into operation four years prior to the *Star Ariel*'s disappearance. Designed as a compromise airplane, with the wings of the Royal Air Force Lancaster bomber and a roomy commercial fuselage, it had been successively redesigned and developed as Britain's principal competitor to American DC-4's and Constellations in transatlantic commercial aviation.

In December 1948 it was announced that BSAA had received a full certificate of the airworthiness of Tudor IV's after extensive modifications to fuselage and engines.

After five days of covering the Atlantic search area section by section without turning up a single clue, the U.S. Air Force announced that the hunt was abandoned as of January 22. According to spokesmen at Hamilton, Bermuda, "It was necessary to give up the search because both planes and personnel were nearing the exhaustion point."

The *Star Ariel* was the second plane within the short period of one month to disappear without a trace in the "Limbo of the Lost." The other lost craft was a DC-3 airliner on a flight from San Juan to Miami. The hunt for her was called off, without finding a single clue, 12 days earlier on January 10, 1949.

The investigation of the disappearance went on for almost a year, but no evidence as to what had happened was uncovered.

The following information has been extracted from the report by the Chief Inspector of Accidents, Air Commodore Vernon Brown, which was published on December 20, 1949. (M.C.A.P. 78, H. M. Stationery Office, 3s net), states: "Through lack of evidence due to no wreckage having been found the cause of the accident to the *Star Ariel* is unknown.

"The *Star Ariel* was lost almost exactly a year after a sister aircraft, the *Star Tiger,* had disappeared in much the same area in equally mysterious circumstances.

"These two losses led to the withdrawal of the Tudor IV's for carrying passengers, and they have not been employed for this purpose by the corporation since, even though they have operated successfully on the Berlin air-lift and elsewhere."

In his report on the *Star Ariel,* Air Commodore Brown stated there was no evidence of defect in, or failure of, any part of the aircraft or its equipment before its departure from Bermuda. The pilot was experienced on the route; the radio officer was very experienced and dependable and above average in being able to effect instrument repairs, and he also was experienced on this crossing; good radio communication had been maintained with the aircraft up to and including receipt of its last message; there were no weather complications, and a study of weather reports gives no reason to believe that the accident was due to meteorological conditions. There was also no evidence of sabotage.

It appeared the *Star Ariel* had joined her sister aircraft, *Star Tiger* and the DC-3 charter flight in the record book of unsolved mysteries of the "Limbo of the Lost."

British South American Airways' main mission was divided between serving Bermuda, the West Indies, and the west coast of South America.

Avro Lancastrians opened the BSAA route on September 2, 1946, and were replaced by the ill-fated Tudor IV's a year later on October 31.

As I pointed out in the preceding story of the *Star Ariel,* not only were the Tudor IV's withdrawn from service but this last disappearance without a satisfactory explanation was the straw that broke the airlines back.

The British mid-Atlantic service was not resumed until March 2, 1950, when BOAC (which by that time had taken over BSAA) opened a Constellation service via Bermuda.

In the interim, a connection had been maintained by way of New York, Bermuda, and Nassau to Kingston, Panama, and Lima, with British York transport planes based at Nassau. Constellations continued to provide the service, which was extended from Nassau to Santiago, Chile, between October 1950 and May 1, 1951. Not until March 5, 1952 was the longer route via Gander, Newfoundland, reintroduced. Then the Caribbean once again was reached as an extension of the main North Atlantic services.

Among the missing on the *Star Ariel* were:

R. Demire Quesada—Peruvian
Miss J. Muntalvo—Spanish
E. Murchard—British
T. Duboisson—British
F. Burthroyd—British

Mrs. R. Bentham Green—British
Miss J. Hodge—British
E. Stevens—British
H. S. Stewart—British
Group Captain H. Saker—British
Mrs. Marshall Meade and 2-year-old son—Jamaican

The names of six crew members were given as:

J. McPhee, Captain, Pilot
F. Dauncey, First Officer
V. Shapley, Second Officer
G. Rettie, Radio Officer
K. Coleman, Steward
J. Moxon, Stewardess

# The Disappearance of the 4-Engine Navy Super-Constellation October 30, 1954

## Passengers and crew missing: 42

Forty-two people, including four women and five children, took off in a four-engine Navy Super-Constellation from Patuxent River Naval Air Station, Maryland. After two and a half hours of flying, the pilot reported that he would have to return to Patuxent Station because of mechanical trouble.

When they landed, another Super-Constellation was pressed into service, and at 9:39 P.M., Saturday, October 30, 1954, the 42 people were back in the air. Next stop was scheduled for Lagens, the Azores, and then on to Port Lyautey, Africa.

At 11:00 P.M. a routine position report was received placing the triple-tailed transport at a point more than

350 miles off the Maryland coast. That was the last word to be heard from the military passenger plane.

Air-sea search operations got underway at 1:00 A.M., after the four-engine plane failed to make two scheduled hourly contacts with shore.

Joining the hunt were planes and ships from up and down the eastern seaboard, Bermuda, the Azores, and the Mediterranean. Also included in the search were aircraft carriers and destroyers.

Search conditions were reported as generally favorable. It was partly cloudy with light winds in the ribbon of ocean area where the hunt was conducted. The weather bureau in New York reported that the water temperatures along the search route ranged from the mid-50s up.

Planes and ships with special radar for night operations pressed on with the search. The Navy said the plane was equipped with 5 20-man life rafts, 102 life vests, 90 exposure suits, emergency radio, and a signal pistol with 12 shells.

In operational command of the search was Vice Admiral Laurence T. DuBose, Commander of the Eastern Sea Frontier. His office reported that about 200 planes and 30 surface vessels, including the aircraft carrier *Leyte*, were concentrated in a 120-mile path that stretched from the Maryland coast to the Azores.

A B-29 rescue plane flew from Prestwick, Scotland, to join in the hunt. Slung under its fuselage was a completely equipped 15-man life raft that could be dropped into the ocean from an altitude of 800 feet and guided by remote control to any survivors who might be sighted.

The missing Super-Constellation had enough fuel on

board to stay in the air until 10 A.M., October 31. Flying time to the Azores ordinarily took about nine hours. There was hope that the pilot somehow managed to ditch safely and that survivors had time to climb onto life rafts.

Planes and ships crisscrossed and recrossed the area in a scientific pattern that covered about a million square miles. Every yard of the search area was scanned by sight and radar every six hours.

Numerous reports of debris, oil, and a faint SOS were received. Captain Ray Needham, Naval rescue coordinator for the area said that all reports received were checked out but there had been "no valid sightings."

At 3:00 P.M., Wednesday, November 3, the Navy gave orders to abandon the search for the Super-Constellation. Vice Admiral DuBose informed reporters, "The search was called off because of extreme weather conditions."

The search for the missing Super-Constellation was suddenly renewed on November 6 in the hope of finding some physical clue to the cause of the tragedy.

No life rafts or bodies or debris were ever found. Once again another plane flew into the "Limbo of the Lost."

Aboard the ill fated Navy Super-Constellation were 32 naval personnel and 2 members of the Air Force. Half of the 21 air crewmen were slated to leave the flight at the Azores to pick up another plane. Seven of the eight civilians aboard were wives or children of service men. Crew member and passenger lists were as follows:

*Crew Members:*

Lieut. Comdr. John S. Cole—Md.
Hospitalman 3/C John T. Davis—W. Va.
Aviation metalsmith 2/C Gerald F. DeBoid—Md.
Lieut. Herbert W. Eden—Md.
Airman Frank J. Graziano—Pa.
Chief Machinist's Mate Eugene Huntley—Md.
Lieut. Russell L. Klemetti—Md.
Lieut. John G. Leonard—Md.
Chief Machinist's Mate Frank T. Meidl—Md.
Aviation radioman 2/C Raymond R. Meyers—Ill.
Hospitalman 3/C Noel R. Moore—Pa.
Lieut. Peter J. Mostika—Md.
James R. Pflager—Md.
Seaman Florence B. Reitkrentz—Wis.
Johnny M. Roberts—Kans.
Lieut. Davis Roberts—Tenn.
Lieut. Rodney S. Sprigg, Jr.—Md.
Seaman Louis H. Staley, Jr.—Md.
Chief Machinist's Mate Robert Stephenson—N.J.
Machinist's mate Robert T. Thomas—Md.
Seaman Marian L. Wolff—Calif.

*Passengers:*

Lieut. Gilbert Jacobson of Brooklyn, N.Y., en route on
   Navy assignment to Port Lyautey with his wife and twin
   2-year-old children.
Major Edward H. Adrian—Pa.
Chief dental technician Francis Earl Baker—Va.
Ensign Cornelius P. Collins—N.Y.
Radioman, first class John Edward Gregg—Kans.
David R. Harr—Port Lyautey, North Africa
Geraldine L. Harr—Port Lyautey, North Africa
Kathy A. Harr—Port Lyautey, North Africa
Timothy J. Harr—Port Lyautey, North Africa
Seaman Leonard Rey Hawvaker—Iowa
Major Joseph U. Herold—APO 117
Dental Technician Valentine Muscarelli—Va.
George W. Pongonis, Jr.—N.J.
Chief Machinist's Mate Robert L. Ridle—Calif.
Ronald Larue Warren—Pa.
Billy Joe Wayne—W. Va.

Apprentice Seaman George Owen Willingham—N.C.
Apprentice Seaman James White—Pa.


## Navy Seaplane Hunted, Friday, November 9, 1956

### Missing crew members: 10

A U.S. Navy, Martin Marlin P5M, twin-engined patrol flying boat with seven enlisted men and three officers aboard was reported as missing Friday night, November 9, 1956. The plane, assigned to Squadron 49 Naval Station in Bermuda, radioed a last position report as 350 miles north of its home station at 8:30 P.M.

When the Martin's next position reports were not received, a search by air and sea craft was ordered, but without any great haste; after all, the missing craft was a seaplane and if anything had happened to its engines the pilot would just simply sit down on the sea and await rescue. According to officials, the aircraft had enough fuel to have stayed aloft until six-thirty in the morning.

Then a message from the Liberian freighter, the *Captain Lyras,* changed the whole tempo of the hunt. She reported seeing a plane in flames over the Atlantic Ocean at a point about 400 miles east-southeast of New York City at 9:15 P.M.

Coast Guard aircraft from Quonset Point, Rhode Island and Floyd Bennett Field, Brooklyn; four other P5M's stationed in Bermuda, two P2V Neptune patrol bombers from Maryland, plus two Navy destroyers and the Coast Guard cutter *Chincoteague* proceeded to the area given by the *Captain Lyras*. At the time the *Chincoteague* was alerted, she was 180 miles from the *Captain Lyras* on her way to Norfolk, Virginia, with 33 men from the German freighter *Helga Bolten*. They were rescued from the 10,000-dead-weight-ton vessel which developed trouble some 400 miles off Newfoundland.

Shortly after the initial report of the sighting of the burning aircraft, the *Captain Lyras* radioed that it had seen what appeared to be a life raft with a light on it about four miles away. However, the freighter lost sight of the raft in the darkness. The freighter reported that she would stand by with all the crew looking out.

As the first aircraft and cutter arrived at the scene, flares were dropped and a quick search was conducted, yet no wreckage or life rafts were sighted.

The aviation weather forecast at the New York International Airport, Idlewild, said that a cold front was in the vicinity, which was about 380 miles north-northwest of Bermuda, with winds about 33 miles per hour. Navy craft at the search area reported scattered clouds at 1,000 feet, showers but good visibility, and moderate seas. If anything was out there they would find it.

Meanwhile, the joint sea-air search was placed under the coordination of the Navy's Eastern Sea Frontier Command in New York. The Commandant, Vice Admiral Frederick W. McMahon, was quoted as declaring the Navy plane "may or may not" be the alleged sighted burning craft. A check by the Coast Guard, the Military Air Transport Service, and the Civil Aeronautics Administration's communications center revealed that no other planes had been reported missing or in trouble.

The mystery became even more clouded when the Coast Guard reported that a ship in the vicinity of the *Captain Lyras* released information about seeing a plane flying overhead and had flashed a large spotlight on it; however, the plane was not in trouble. There was a good possibility that the light on the plane might have been seen by the *Captain Lyras* and mistaken for flames.

Again hope was raised as Naval aircraft and surface ships were dispatched to a point 300 miles northwest of Bermuda after the Spanish freighter *Astro* reported sighting a white flare in the area at six o'clock, Sunday night. Nothing was found.

The Navy and Coast Guard air and surface craft continued their search between Bermuda and Rhode Island, day and night, until Tuesday, November 13, when the hunt was officially called off.

Another craft with its entire crew entered into the oblivion of the "Limbo of the Lost" without giving its hunters a radio signal or a visible clue to work on.

The Department of the Navy in Washington announced that the following men were aboard the plane, and that as of Saturday, November 10 they were officially listed as missing:

Petty Officer 3/C Wendell F. Beverly—Williamstown, Mass.
Petty Officer 3/C Billy G. Comer—Blossburg, Ala.
Petty Officer 3/C Jesse W. Grable—Centralia, Ill.
Petty Officer 3/C Richard W. Montgomery—Cynwyd, Pa.
Lieut. (j.g.) Charles W. Patterson—Bermuda
Petty Officer 2/C Lyle F. Quimby—Minneapolis, Minn.
Lieut. (j.g.) Cyrus E. Reid, Jr.—Dallas, Tex.

Petty Officer 1/C Robert W. Taylor—West Liberty, Ohio
Comdr. John M. Sweeney—Warwick, Bermuda
Airman Bobbie L. Sanders—Houston, Tex.

## KB-50 Tanker Vanishes,
## Monday, January 8, 1962
### Missing crew members: 9

At approximately one o'clock on the afternoon of Monday, January 8, 1962, the control tower at Langley Air Force Base, Virginia, received a radio position report from a KB-50J refueling tanker which had taken off from the base at 11:17 A.M.

Command pilot Major Tawney reported his plane's position as about 240 miles east of Norfolk, Virginia, estimated time of arrival at Lajes, in the Azores: 6:52 P.M.

When the Air Force tanker failed to contact Langley tower as scheduled at 2:00 P.M., the all-too-familiar emergency call was made to Coast Guard air-sea rescue headquarters:

"United States Air Force KB-50 tanker plane . . . converted bomber with four piston engines and two jets . . . believed down at sea . . . nine men aboard . . . enough fuel to stay aloft until about midnight."

An air-sea search was concentrated along a path 130 miles wide, running east from the missing plane's last reported position. Weather reports in the area: "windy but good, with visibility ten miles."

Among the planes participating in the hunt were 32 C-130 turbine-propeller cargo aircraft out of Langley,

48

2 Coast Guard Grumman Albatross amphibians based in Bermuda, and 3 Martin Mariner flying boats from Elizabeth City, North Carolina.

Surface vessels in the special search effort included the Coast Guard cutters *Escanaba, Campbell,* and *Ingham,* plus all merchant ships at sea in the vicinity of the widespread hunt.

After five days, the Coast Guard headquarters, which coordinated the search operations, called the air-sea rescue search off, having exhausted every possibility of locating the KB-50 and its crew. According to officials not one single clue was found.

Officials at Langley Air Force Base released the names of these missing crewmen:

Maj. Robert J. Tawney, Pilot—Middletown, Ohio
Capt. Bernard A. Hanley, Navigator—Jersey City, N.J.
M/Sgt. Arnold W. Womak, Flight Eng.—Rossville, Ga.
T/Sgt. Harry Stetser, Crew Chief—Donora, Pa.
S/Sgt. Billie D. Moore, Refueling Tech.—Tulsa, Okla.
A/3C William J. Anderson, Assistant Crew Chief—San Bernardino, Calif.
A/2C Carlton A. Link, Refueling Spec.—Tampa, Fla.
A/2C Paul M. Clawson, Refueling Spec.—Pacific, Calif.
1st Lt. Zoltan R. F. Szaloki, Copilot—Whitinsville, Mass.

# Hunt on for Lost
# C-133 Cargomaster,
# Sunday, September 22, 1963

### Missing crew members: 10

It seemed the "Limbo of the Lost" was once again the victor in the sea search for a four-engine Air Force C-133 Cargomaster, lost on a flight between Dover, Delaware, and Terceira Island, the Azores.

The plane with 10 men on board vanished Sunday, September 22, 1963, after the pilot gave his last position report at 3:00 A.M. as 88 miles southeast of Cape May, New Jersey.

A 23-plane rescue fleet scanned a 640-mile zone, east from the coast between Atlantic City, New Jersey, to Virginia Beach, Virginia. Many times search aircraft flew as low as 400 to 600 feet, in parallel east-west tracks covering 80 by 40 miles of ocean, 180 miles southeast of Cape May.

As search planes flew their assigned low-level courses, 2 Coast Guard aircraft circled above at 26,000 feet, coordinating the effort and relaying radio messages between the search planes and their home bases.

On the afternoon of Wednesday, September 25, Captain James L. Smith of Nahunta, Georgia—pilot of a five-man, twin-engine Grumman amphibian—was ordered from his half-searched area to an adjacent sector to his west. Upon arrival at the target he spent several hours circling and dropping smoke markers to guide a Coast Guard cutter to debris. After close examination

50

UNSOLVED
MYSTERIES
FROM THE
"LIMBO OF
THE LOST"

## COLLIER OVERDUE A MONTH

### Vessel With 293 Persons Aboard Last Heard From on March 4.

**WAS THEN IN WEST INDIES**

### Touched at Port There on Her Way from Brazil with a Cargo of Manganese.

**RADIO SEARCH UNAVAILING**

### Ship in Command of Naval Reserve—Consul Gottschalk and Many Men Aboard.

*Special to The New York Times.*

WASHINGTON, April 14.—The Navy ment announced tonight that the val collier Cyclops, 's United States officers and 221 gers, and a cargo n missing since arch 13. The an- to the probability r or submarine has hin the last month Cuba and the coast for the safety of the 200 persons on board ned.

Department is satis- yclops has been lost is fact that before an- this afternoon the names t and men on board the artment in its messages to hin informed them of its e Cyclops w passengers Alfred L. s New York Consul Gen- Brasil, and wa States from his ssenger list ir partments contain g Gottschalk, Co

---

## 'Plane Afire' Report Stirs Atlantic Hunt

A widespread search by air and sea was in progress early today after a Liberian freighter reported seeing a plane in flames over the Atlantic Ocean at a point about 400 miles east-southeast of New York City.

An SOS message from the freighter, the Captain Lyras, was intercepted by the Coast Guard at 8:51 o'clock last night. The message, which said that it had seen "a plane overhead in flames," was also picked up by three or four vessels near the scene. They proceeded to the area to begin a search.

So far as could be learned, no civilian or military plane had been reported either missing or in trouble by early this morning.

Three Coast Guard

---

## MORE SHIPS ADDED TO MYSTERY LIST

### Almost Simultaneous Disappearance Without a Trace Regarded as Significant.

**FOUL PLAY IN DEERING CASE**

### State Department Goes on Record as Suspecting It in the Fate of the Crew.

*Special to The New York Times.*

WASHINGTON, June 21.—The names of three other vessels which have disappeared off the Atlantic coast of the United States in mysterious circumstances were added by the Department of Commerce today to the list of those whose failure to appear is attributed by the Government to circumstances more or less related to the supposed kidnapping or murder of the crew of the American schooner Carroll A. Deering off Dia- Shoals, North Carolina, last Jan

It is not asserted that all of the vessels were the victims of pirates, or possibly Bolshevist sympathizers, intending to dispose of ships and cargoes to the Government of Soviet but the fact that all these ves appeared at about the same time, none of them left a trace significant.

The missing ships disappeared southern Atlantic Coast. Three of them sailed from out the same time. Ordi that disappear leave some the way of boats, wreck bodies, but it is said that hips added to the list today whatever. They were as the Ger- the effort of their elab no tell-tale vestige of they sent to the bot-

of Yate and Albyan. vessels whose disappear e Governr once they hipping ond she steam byan. 1920. for he 240 to overnm ut to able pn N She ot th

---

## THE NEW YORK TIMES

## U.S. Fuel Plane Lost

Planes and ships searched yesterday for an Air Force KB- refueling plane missing on ight from Langley Air F Va., to les, in the res. Nine men were aboard. y early evening not a single had been reported to Coast nd headquarters here, which co ordinating the search opera

plane, a converted bomber four piston engines and sts, too of at 11:17 A. M lade its scheduled hourly eport an hour after take- ring its position as 240 last of Norfolk.

the cov
General to Como m
Britain and France previously had agreed to get out of Suez Canal areas so that the United Nations command could assume supervision over the two-day-old cease-fire in Egypt.
Maj. Gen.
Cana
new
the E
expect
this w
with E
The
uing a
tween 30
be joined
units fr
India. Fl

was the last heard from craft.

The plane was due in Azores at 6:52 P. M. M It had enough fuel to re aloft until shortly bef midnight Monday.

The search concentrated alo a 130-mile-wide path runnir from the missing plane last position Weather in the area wa reported with visibility ten miles, good ing in the search were thirty 130 cargo planes turbine-propeller two Coast Guard Grumman Al-

### ENDS AIRMEN SEARCH

### Navy Gives Up Hunt for Lost Nine Men Off Miami Coast

MIAMI, Fla., Dec. 10 (AP)—The Navy today called off its mammoth special search for twenty-seven Navy airmen who disappeared in six planes Wednesday.

"Planes and surface craft which travel the area where the airmen are believed to have disappeared will remain on the alert indefinite ," the Navy reported, "but the ended as of

---

## THE NEW YORK TIMES, SUNDAY

## SEARCH PRESSED FOR NAVY PLANE

### Patrol Craft With 10 Aboard Believed One Seen Aflame Near Bermuda Friday

patrol plane t was being Navy and in waters

ed to be y freighter in Friday

cepted another message from the freighter at 9:15 o'clock re- porting that an explosion had been heard and felt strongly aboard the vessel. Still another message from the freighter re- ported the sighting about four miles away of what appeared to be a life raft with a light on it. The freighter's report added, however, that the raft had be- come obscured by rain, heavy seas and darkness.

According to the Navy, weather conditions at the time of the SOS were scattered clouds at 1,500 feet, showers with good visibility and moderate seas.

The joint sea-air being coordinated the Navy's Easte tier Command and her ick W. McMahon, w declaring the Navy or may not" be the a Other Naval authori folk, Va., and in Bern

---

## FEAR FREIGHTER WAS LOST.

### Owners of the Suduffco Ask Help in Search—29 Men Aboard.

The Transmarine Corporation of Port Newark, N. J., announced yes- terday that it had requested the Navy Department to search for its freighter Suduffco. Officials of the company fear for the safety of the freighter Suduffco, which sailed from Port ninety-nine and

The Navy's Lyras— reported mes" at

missing craft.

The miss "Marlin" flying boa carrying s three offic said the last positio Friday wh of the

The U Tin tion in Be is assigne 49, respon position

sum loan, of Dec. 31, 1951 policy of the the borrower principal only on credit as he uses. per cent over the period, w $3,750,0 is available to be dra

The NEW YORK TIMES

Headline stories on disappearances in Bermuda Triangle

WIDE WORLD

British plane "Star Tiger" radioed its position and mysteriously disappeared.

British airliner "Ariel", departed for Chile with 20 aboard, and vanished.

Freighter "Sandra" sailed from Savannah for Venezuela with crew of 12 and was never heard from.

Five torpedo planes on training flight never returned. A PBM rescue plane with 13 aboard also was lost.

Plane carrying 32 persons flew nearly 1000 miles toward Miami but never arrived.

Map showing last recorded position of 9 planes and 1 ship lost in "The Devil's Triangle"

Ghost ship *Gloria Colita* was found abandoned in the Gulf of Mexico in February 1940, with no trace of her crew of 9.

Collier U.S.S. *Cyclops* disappeared completely off British West Indies 3/13/18. There were over 300 persons aboard.

Tudor IV airliner, like *Star Tiger* and *Star Ariel*, sister ships lost off Bermuda in 1948 and 1949. The reasons for these mysterious disappearances have still to be found.

## JANUARY 31 1948

# 31 MISSING IN AIR LINER

## NOW "PRESUMED LOST"

### ALL-DAY SEARCH OFF BERMUDA

The British South American Airways' Tudor IV aircraft Star Tiger, reported missing yesterday, with 25 passengers and a crew of six on board, on its way to Bermuda, is now presumed lost, according to a Ministry of Civil Aviation statement issued last night.

The aircraft, which was due at Hamilton, Bermuda, at 6 o'clock yesterday morning—it left the Azores on Thursday afternoon—last reported its position in a routine wireless message as 380 miles north-east of Bermuda.

#### FROM OUR CORRESPONDENT

BERMUDA, JAN. 30

Seventeen aircraft were searching a wide area of the Atlantic to-day for traces of the Star Tiger. The air liner's last radio message was a routine report at 11.15 p.m. giving her position as 440 miles north-east of Bermuda. No distress signals were sent, nor was there any hint of trouble.

The first search machine left at 3.15 this morning. A coordinated search was conducted by the United States naval operating base at Bermuda, with the help of civilian aircraft. Rescue and search units from Newfoundland and along the Atlantic coast also cooperated, and the search will continue until wreckage or survivors are sighted.

Fifteen hours after the search started no trace had been found, and it was reported that the weather was squally and visibility "low."

### INQUIRY ORDERED

The Ministry of Civil Aviation announced last night that a public inquiry would be held

## JANUARY 18 1949

# 29 IN MISSING AIR-LINER

## STAR ARIEL OVERDUE FROM BERMUDA

### From Our Correspondent

BERMUDA, JAN. 17

A British South American Airways air-liner on its way from Bermuda to Kingston, Jamaica, is missing over the Atlantic. It left Bermuda at 8 o'clock this morning. The pilot is Captain J. C. McPhee.

The aircraft was on a regular flight from London Airport to Jamaica, and Bermuda was the last stop on the journey.

The following statement was issued in London early this morning:—

"B.S.A.A. regrets to announce that the corporation's aircraft Star Ariel, which left London for Santiago, Chile, on Saturday, is overdue on passage between Bermuda and Kingston, Jamaica. The aircraft, which left Bermuda at about 1230 G.M.T. yesterday (Monday) and was due at Kingston at 1802 hours G.M.T., was carrying, so far as is known at present, 22 passengers and a crew of seven.

"The last message received rom the aircraft was dispatched about an hour after leaving Bermuda. Air-sea rescue operations are in progress."

Five British passengers for Kingston and two for Santiago boarded the machine at London airport.

MIAMI, JAN. 17.—An air rescue aircraft from Findley Field, Bermuda, searched the area over which the Star Ariel was travelling without finding any trace of it.

New York coastguard officials said that rescue machines from Salem, Massachusetts, Brooklyn, New York, and Elizabeth City, North Carolina, would go to Bermuda to-night to join searchers to-morrow.—*Reuter.*

❖ Thirty-one people—six crew and 25 passengers—lost their lives when the Tudor IV Star Tiger disappeared between the Azores and Bermuda in January, 1948. All Tudor IV aircraft were then grounded for reliability trials and did not return to the Bermuda run for 11

All contact with the *Marine Sulphur Queen* was lost 2/4/63.

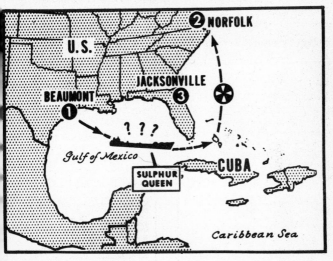

*Sulphur Queen's* last message was sent about 200 miles off
Key West, Fla. Later, search yielded only bits of debris.

Lost training mission: 5 Navy TBM's left Ft. Lauderdale for Bahamas 12/5/45. They never arrived. PBM Martin Mariner, sent to rescue, also vanished. Crew of 27 was lost.

Nuclear-powered sub U.S.S. *Scorpion* sank 460 miles off the Azores, May 1968. No certain cause for disaster is known.

Admiral Thomas H. Moorer shows location of the *Scorpion*.

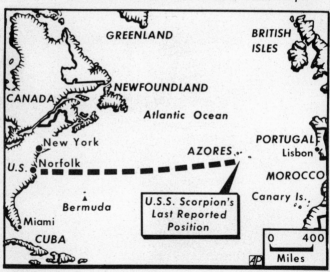

Last message from sub was 5/21/68. Crew of 99 was aboard.

Famous ghost ship *Mary Celeste*, found abandoned in 1872.

The Sargasso Sea, long the subject of sailors' myths, has been known since antiquity as "The Port of Missing Ships."

Does this photo really show the fabled Loch Ness Monster?

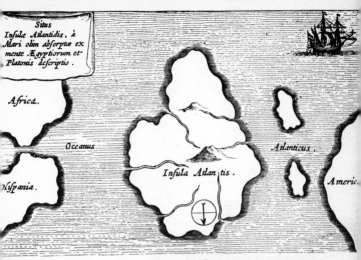

Lost Continent of Atlantis, as seen in 17th-century print.

Tales of sea monsters abound in the "Limbo of the Lost."

Sea serpent presumably sighted by the *British Banner* in 1860.

The Flying Dutchman, part of sea folklore since mid-1600s.

of the wreckage, it turned out to be of no significance.

A Coast Guard spokesman said search planes sighted pieces of brown and blue metal objects about 2 feet square, partially submerged, some blue cloth, and a 3-foot round, light brown object in some 6 locations, all within a 30-mile radius about 440 miles east of Cape May, New Jersey. The spokesman said that from the description of the round object it could have been the fuselage of the missing plane.

Two Coast Guard cutters and three Navy destroyers were sent to the area to examine the wreckage. In the meantime, the widespread hunt was called off, pending examination of the find.

The Coast Guard, acting as the search and rescue coordinator, reordered the special air-sea search to continue after examination of all the discovered debris proved that it was not part of the missing aircraft. They pointed out that hope of finding survivors looked grim.

As the day's hunt ended on Wednesday, September 25, the decision was made to abandon all hope for the 10 men. Many searchers expressed sadness, not wanting to give up, although some said they held little real hope because of high winds and seas that plagued the search area Monday, September 23.

Major Robert W. Griswold, a search squadron briefing officer, summed up the situation: "The factors that must be weighed included the number of hours a plane is missing, the areas that have been covered and a judgment based on past experience. You've got to stop sometime."

When conducting a search, definite "standard operating procedures" are closely followed by air-sea rescue personnel. Clues to the whereabouts or fate of the hunted can be quickly uncovered if the area of the last known approximate or projected position of a missing craft is searched thoroughly and quickly.

Search personnel are trained to spot floating debris, oil slicks, large schools of fish (shark or barracuda), life saving craft, and floating bodies, dead or alive.

Under no circumstances will an evaluation of a possible clue be determined from a distance. Assistance must be called in for close-up analysis of a suspect target.

What follows is an excellent example of how an air-sea rescue search is conducted.

## The Disappearance That Didn't Take Place
### Wednesday, August 28, 1963
#### Missing crew members: 11

Two Strategic Air Command KC-135A Stratotankers roared off the runway of Homestead Air Force Base, south of Miami, on the morning of Wednesday, August 28, 1963. The four-engine jets, Air Force versions of Boeing's 707 passenger airliners, were scheduled for a routine aerial refueling mission between Bermuda and the Bahamas. The skies were clear, ideal flying weather for the delicate rendezvous job.

At noon the tankers contacted Homestead tower with a routine position report, approximately 300 miles southwest of Bermuda. When the big jets were reported as overdue and could not be contacted by radio, once again the air-sea rescue alert was sounded.

Ths missing KC-135's had a range of 4,500 miles and a cruising speed of 600 miles per hour. According to projected figures, they had enough fuel to stay in the air until approximately 6:00 P.M.

Throughout the night searchers covered the region of the downed crafts' last known position. The next day, Thursday, August 29, one of the search planes, a C-54 out of Bermuda, reported an oil slick about 350 miles southwest of Bermuda. A ship also reported finding a life jacket in the same vicinity.

Coast Guard search headquarters announced, after examining the reported items, that they definitely were not from the missing KC-135's.

The merchant ship *Azalea City,* out of Wilmington, Delaware, retrieved a flight helmet stenciled "Gardner" and other items, including three rubber life rafts of the type carried by the tankers, several life jackets, and an exposure suit. The Coast Guard cutter *Owasco* from New London, Connecticut, also picked up debris over a wide area in the same vicinity, 300 miles southwest of Bermuda.

Spokesmen at the Air Rescue Service Headquarters, Orlando, Florida, said that a ten-square-mile "floating junkyard" of debris had come from at least one of the two missing tankers. No survivors were spotted, however, and the fate of the crewmen appeared dim.

Two HU-16B Grumman Albatross amphibian planes sighted a second concentration of wreckage on Friday, August 30, 160 miles from the "floating junkyard" of debris. The new find was 400 miles east of Fort Pierce, Florida, but sea conditions prevented the planes from landing.

Air Force officials said that a Coast Guard cutter was en route, and if the debris was that of the second jet tanker it would appear to conflict with a theory that the jets had collided. They went on to say the latest discovery spurred new hope into the massive air-sea rescue search for possible survivors.

Shortly after the cutter arrived at the scene, air-sea command received a report that the debris was not of the missing KC-135. Nothing more than on old buoy in a patch of dark seaweed was found.

After five days of scouring the Atlantic for survivors, the Air Force gave up the search. They announced that wreckage found in the ocean 300 miles southwest of Bermuda by search ships and planes had been determined definitely to have come from the 2 missing KC-135 Stratotankers and that the debris would be sent to Homestead Air Force Base for study. Apparently both planes crashed together in mid-air, instantly killing all 11 crewmen.

In the procedures of air-sea rescue in full operation, a hunt always begins by working on the assumption that a craft could not break up at sea without leaving many telltale clues such as floating debris, large oil slicks, lifesaving gear, and floating bodies. Some, or all, will always turn up. If not found at sea, many times they will wash ashore.

When a ditching at sea occurs, emergency signaling equipment such as radios (voice or code), flares, and mirrors have been provided as standard equipment on lifesaving boats and rafts since the early 1940s.

Names of missing crew members were listed as follows:

*Plane One:*
Capt. Allen C. Ferguson, 29, Pilot—Elgin, Ill.

Capt. Donald G. Edson, 30—(no address available)
Capt. Julius O. Womack, 30—Pioneer, La.
Capt. Gerald Gardner, 28—Lincoln, Nebr.
1st Lt. Melvin C. Pump, 29—(no address available)
T/Sgt. Raymond L. Fish, 30—LaCrosse, Wis.

*Plane Two:*
Capt. Richard A. Larson, 34, Pilot—Minneapolis, Minn.
Capt. Keith R. Goffin, 29—Bellevue, Ill.
1st Lt. William E. Smith, 26—Memphis, Tenn.
M/Sgt. Carl H. Burris, 39—Danube, Calif.
S/Sgt. Lyle E. Overlees, 25—Fulda, Minn.

# III

## Vanishing Steamships

# Navy Collier *Cyclops*
# Missing, March 13, 1918

## Passengers and crew lost: 309

The big 14,500-ton American Naval fuel-supply ship, U.S.S. *Cyclops* was reported overdue at her Atlantic port of destination, Norfolk, Virginia. Navy Department officials said the 540-foot collier, built in 1910 and considered the last word in marine construction, steamed from Bahia, Brazil on January 28, 1918, with a cargo of manganese, much needed by the allied nations at war with Germany.

First stop scheduled on the long voyage was Georgetown, British West Indies, on March 3, to take on coal. The following day she headed out to sea, bound for Norfolk, but with one of her two engines damaged. Naval authorities quickly pointed out that the *Cyclops* had enough power to be driven at ten knots an hour, even with one engine. In any event, the engine problem would not have prevented the collier from communicating by radio. If her main engines were totally disabled, the big ship would still be capable of using her radio plant.

The only civilian listed among the passengers was the United States Consul-General at Rio de Janeiro. Other passengers were two U.S. Marine lieutenants, 70 Naval enlisted men returning to the United States, plus the ship's crew of 15 Naval reserve officers and 221 enlisted personnel.

At the peak of World War I, on January 8, 1918, the *Cyclops* had been detached from her Atlantic fleet group at Virginia and assigned to the Overseas Transport Service with the U.S. Navy.

When the big supply ship was reported as missing, Secretary of the Navy Daniels ordered an unremitting search of trade routes by American and French Naval and Merchant vessels. He ordered that every quarter, every rod of the *Cyclops'* route be covered; every one of the scores of islands and isolated bays be entered, and every beach which dots that portion of the sea be scrutinized.

At a press conference, Mr. Daniels' chief assistant reported, "Hope is still felt by the Navy. We refuse to give up the search until every possibility of finding some trace of the collier has been exhausted."

Although a thorough search was conducted of the probable course the big ship would have followed, not a trace of information concerning her had been obtained. Radio calls from every possible point were beamed to the *Cyclops,* but to no avail. Every day of the search only resulted in deepening the mystery.

On April 16, a spokesman from the Office of the Secretary of the Navy reported, "No well-founded reason can be given to explain the *Cyclops* being overdue. We refuse to believe that the collier could have been wiped out without leaving a trace."

For the first time since the hunt began, the Navy officially went on record as saying, "The search still continues, but the Navy feels extremely anxious as to the safety of the *Cyclops* and her 309 passengers and crew."

Explanations for the collier's disappearance were offered from every quarter and covered a variety of suggestions.

## 1. Sub-raider or floating mine

There were many advocates of the theory that the *Cyclops* struck a floating mine, or that a German U-boat was responsible for her disappearance.

A Navy Department statement read, "There have been no reports that would indicate the presence of either submarines or mines in the locality of the *Cyclops'* route. Further, certainly debris or lifeboats would have been found." After the war, German Admiralty records revealed that no submarines had been in the waters of the West Indies during March and April of 1918.

## 2. Hurricane or severe storm

It was admitted that the possibility of a sudden hurricane, not infrequent in those waters, might have first disabled and then engulfed the *Cyclops*.

According to official records, there were no reports of a hurricane or stormy weather conditions in the area in which the collier would have had to pass. Even if such a disaster did occur, why wasn't any debris found?

## 3. Hijacking

The conjecture that enemy agents might have gained control in a midnight mutiny was imposed.

Naval officials said that even in such a well-nigh

impossible event, lack of coal would have prevented an attempt to start on a long transatlantic voyage. Further, German Admiralty records captured after the war did not indicate the occurrence of such a plot.

## 4. Explosion

Another theory offered was that an internal explosion, such as a time bomb, might have destroyed the vessel's wireless and motive power at one instant, or the manganese ore, with which the collier was heavily laden, might, under certain conditions, give off an extremely dangerous gas that exploded.

The Navy Department reported that precautions had been taken against this on all ships engaged in the manganese-carrying trade. If either had happened, the ship itself or surface wreckage would remain to mark her grave.

## 5. Action by traitor

The most vicious explanation offered was that of "traitor"; that the *Cyclops'* captain met, by prearrangement, a German U-Boat and assisted in overpowering the other Americans aboard. This circumstantial accusation was built upon the fact that Lieutenant Commander George W. Worley, of the United States Reserve Force, and captain of the *Cyclops,* was German-born. Also, before he sailed on this last voyage he disposed of some property he owned in Norfolk, Virginia, including the home his wife and daughter lived in. He told friends that when he returned from the voyage he intended to get an extended leave of absence and go back to California and rest. He said he had to have an operation performed and it would take about six months for him to recover his strength.

Worley came to the United States from Germany as a child and was adopted by a man in California. When Worley grew up, he applied to the courts to change his name from George Frederick Wichman to that of the man who had befriended him. In 1893, he became an American citizen.

When this traitor theory was told to Mrs. Worley by reporters, she became very angry. She said her husband was a good American and that his long and faithful record in the government service proved it.

She refused to believe her husband dead; instead she believed the *Cyclops* was probably disabled at sea and that her husband was waiting to be picked up.

In answer to questions about her husband, Mrs. Worley replied, "Do you think my husband would prove a traitor to America, to his wife and little daughter? My husband was and is an American through and through. He hated Germany. He came here seeking freedom and he would fight and die to maintain that freedom. He is just as good an American as any man born in America, and a whole lot better than many of those who question his patriotism now. I hope my husband is alive to settle with his accusers."

The traitor theory was eliminated once and for all when, after the war, it was not supported by captured German Admiralty records.

The U.S.S. *Cyclops* was modern, staunch, well-manned and equipped. To those who are familiar with the sea and navigation, the disappearance of the big collier is inexplicable.

Wreckage of other ships had floated ashore to tell their fate, but no such messenger with a vestige of debris ever arrived to tell the tale of the mysterious disappearance of the *Cyclops*.

The facts surrounding the big ship were released on Thursday, April 11, 1918, almost a month after it had been reported overdue at Norfolk. The U.S. Naval censor requested that the wire press services not publish the information on the grounds that the *Cyclops* had not been given up as lost, and to publish the fact that she was overdue might expose her to submarine or other enemy attack while possibly disabled on the high seas.

The *Cyclops* was finally given up as lost, without explanation, after a month and a half of futile searching, and her name officially stricken from the Naval Register.

Almost eight years later on December 3, 1925, interest in the *Cyclops* was revived in official circles when Secretary Wilbur received from the commandant of the Fifth Naval District a report that the *Orion*, also a Naval collier, had been placed in drydock with hull amidships buckled and twisted, and her forepeak tanks flooded.

The day before, on December 2, the *Orion*, loaded with a cargo of coal, sailed out of Hampton Roads bound for Melville, Rhode Island. Later that same afternoon, just outside the Virginia capes, she encountered stormy weather and was forced to return to port.

As the *Orion* was a sister ship of the *Cyclops*, identical in size and construction, Secretary of the Navy Wilbur ordered a careful inspection and inquiry into the exact cause of the buckling and other damage. He believed whatever caused the trouble could possibly have been linked to the mysterious disappearance of the *Cyclops*. It did not!

At this point we must place the name of the U.S.S *Cyclops* on the list of those in the "Port of Missing Ships" in the "Limbo of the Lost."

## The Freighter *Suduffco* Missing, March 13, 1926

### Missing crew members: 28

The Freighter *Suduffco*, under the command of a Captain T. Turner, sailed from Port Newark, New Jersey, for Los Angeles, California, on March 13, 1926, with a crew of 28. In her hold was a mixed cargo of 4,000 tons, including a large shipment of steel pipe valued at $500,000. She was scheduled to have gone through the Panama Canal on March 22, but never arrived.

On April 7, the Transmarine Corporation of Port Newark, fearing for the safety of the ship and her crew, requested that the Navy Department initiate a search for their missing freighter. They also ordered two of the *Suduffco*'s sister ships into the search—the *Suboatco* took the Gulf of Mexico, and the *Sucaresco* hunted along the West Coast.

An official of the Transmarine Corporation added that, because of the experience of her master, they felt sure the *Suduffco* would be found. Captain Turner commanded ships of the American Line for 25 years, and during World War I had been in charge of an

American transport. He was known as a man who could handle a ship in any situation.

After more than two weeks of searching by the Army, Navy, and Coast Guard in the Atlantic, Gulf of Mexico, and along the West Coast, the Transmarine Corporation announced that as of April 27 the quest had been given up. A company official stated that it was as though the *Suduffco* had been swallowed by a gigantic sea monster.

What happened to the *Suduffco* and her crew will never be known. Nothing has ever been found; therefore we are left no other choice than to place her name on the ghostly honor roll along with those of other ships that have sailed into the "Limbo of the Lost."

# S.S. *Marine Sulphur Queen,* Presumed Lost February 4, 1963

## Missing crew members: 39

The S.S. *Marine Sulphur Queen,* a T2-SE-A1-type tank vessel, under the command of Captain James V. Fanning, steamed out of Beaumont, Texas, on the afternoon of Saturday, February 2, 1963. Her cargo was 15,260 tons of hot, molten sulphur brimstone to be delivered to Norfolk, Virginia, by the afternoon of February 7.

At 1:25 A.M. (EST), about 35 hours after departing Beaumont, the bulk carrier reported its position near Dry Tortugas in the Gulf, 200 miles off Key West, in the straits of Florida. She was operating normally and on schedule. At that time a seaman dispatched a personal radio message regarding some stock

## TREASURY DEPARTMENT
### UNITED STATES COAST GUARD

ADDRESS REPLY TO
**COMMANDANT**
U.S. COAST GUARD
HEADQUARTERS
WASHINGTON 25, D.C.

AUG 23 1969

From: Marine Board of Investigation
To: Commandant (MVI)

Subj: SS MARINE SULPHUR QUEEN; disappearance of at sea on or about 4 February 1963

1. At about 1830, CST, 2 February 1963, the SS MARINE SULPHUR QUEEN, with a crew of 39 and a full cargo of approximately 15,260 long tons of molten sulphur, took departure from Sabine Sea Buoy on a voyage from Beaumont, Texas to Norfolk, Virginia and subsequently disappeared at sea without the transmission of a radio distress message.

2. The SS MARINE SULPHUR QUEEN, O.N. 245295 (Ex-ESSO NEW HAVEN) was an all-welded T2-SE-A1, tankship; of 7240 gross tons and 4057 net tons; length 504 ft., breadth 68.2 ft., and depth 39.2 ft.; built at Sun Shipbuilding and Drydock Co., Chester, Pa. in 1944 and converted to a molten sulphur carrier at Bethlehem Steel Co. Shipyard, Baltimore, Md., during the latter part of 1960. The vessel was single screw, powered by a 7240 shaft horsepower turbo-electric drive manufactured by Westinghouse Elec. & Mfg. Co. The vessel was owned by Marine Sulphur Transport Corporation and operated under a bareboat charter by Marine Transport Lines, Inc., both companies being located at 11 Broadway, New York, N.Y. The conversion to a molten sulphur carrier was accomplished in accordance with plans approved by the U. S. Coast Guard and the American Bureau of Shipping.

3. The vessel was certificated by the U. S. Coast Guard at Baltimore, Md. on 18 January 1961 for the carriage of "Grade E liquids at elevated temperatures" and classed by the American Bureau of Shipping as to hull and machinery. The vessel was recertificated by the U. S. Coast Guard at Beaumont, Texas on 17 January 1963 and retained in class by the American Bureau of Shipping at the same time. The vessel had valid load line certificates, both International and Coastwise, issued by the American Bureau of Shipping and valid radio certificates issued by the Beaumont, Texas office of the Federal Communications Commission covering both the installed radio equipment and the lifeboat portable radio.

purchases. An attempt to send a reply to him went undelivered, as contact could not be made with the *Sulphur Queen.*

When the big tanker didn't report as scheduled at Norfolk, authorities became concerned and tried to establish radio contact with her. No answer.

The situation was reported to air-sea rescue headquarters and a search was launched. Coast Guard vessels and aircraft were dispatched from Virginia, North Carolina, Florida, and Louisiana.

Miami's U.S. Weather Bureau reported that the tanker's course would have taken her through the "Limbo of the Lost" area during a severe Atlantic storm that battered the southeastern coast of the United States with winds of 35 knots.

A Navy patrol plane reported sighting debris 200 miles east of Jacksonville, Florida. Coast Guard officials at Jacksonville Beach said the pilot radioed that the debris consisted of "sticks of wood, several big white objects, and a large amount of yellow substance."

The missing tanker had a white superstructure, but the spokesman would not speculate whether the wreckage might be that of the tanker until an on-the-spot confirmation was made.

Coast Guard patrol boat *Sweet Gum,* was the first to arrive at the scene. Upon close examination, she radioed that the reported debris was definitely not from the *Marine Sulphur Queen.*

It was eight days since any word had been received from the *Queen* and no clues existed, compounding the mystery. The area covered was expanded from Texas to Virginia. Planes and ships ranged as far out as 280 miles into the Atlantic.

Clearing skies over the search area brought out virtually all Coast Guard aircraft stationed along the Atlantic and Gulf coasts. Merchant ships following or crossing the tanker's intended route were asked to report any sign of debris.

But after eight days of scouring the sea, not so much as a sliver of wood belonging to the *Sulphur Queen* had been found. Without any clues and the possibility negative of finding the crew alive, Coast Guard officials abandoned the search.

Board chairman and president of the Marine Transport Corporation, Mr. H. L. White, sent official condolences to the wife of the *Sulphur Queen*'s captain, indicating that the company had given up hope of finding alive the 39-member crew of the missing ship. The telegram received by Mrs. Fanning said the company regretted to inform her that the Coast Guard had given up its search as of February 15, 1963.

Three days later, five widows of the licensed Officers of the lost bulk carrier filed suit in Federal Court asking $2,500,000 damages from the ship's owners.

Unlike the cases of other famous disappearances in the "Limbo of the Lost," some vestiges or flotsam of the *Sulphur Queen* appear to have been found.

On February 20, 1963, a Navy torpedo retriever boat found a life jacket marked "Sulphur Queen" 14 miles southeast of Key West, Florida. Another Coast Guard patrol vessel sent to the area found a second marked life jacket. Immediately an intensive area-wide search was again launched by surface craft and airplanes in hope of finding possible survivors.

Before the new hunt was called off, seven life preservers, one apparently used, four life rings, with a man's shirt attached to one, some pieces of the ship's name board, and miscellaneous debris were found and

brought ashore. A tentative Coast Guard evaluation of
the evidence was that perhaps two crew members
survived and then drowned, or were attacked by sharks
or barracuda.

On Monday, March 24, 1963, a United States Coast
Guard Board of Investigation was convened.

Day after day in the hearing rooms, Coast Guard
Officers searched for clues to the mystery of the *Marine
Sulphur Queen*'s disappearance. Inquiries were
made as to the ship's construction, the properties and
behavior of molten sulphur, and the careful retracing of
the ship's full history. Officials of the Marine Transport
Lines, which owned her, and the men who helped re-
build the old T-2 tanker into a special carrier, took the
stand and added their bits of information, agreeing to
the completeness of the mystery, filling in small pieces.

The investigation of the *Sulphur Queen*'s disappearance brought up possible explanations that were somewhat different from preceding theories regarding disappearances.

## 1. The "Sulphur Queen" was hijacked or captured

Maybe the tanker was hijacked, or she just simply
drifted into Cuban waters and was seized.

If either had happened, word would have been received by the time the air-sea search was called off. This
theory was abandoned.

## 2. It exploded, hit a stray mine, or was sabotaged

Maybe the bulk carrier had exploded, leaking sulphur gas exploded, or possibly she hit a stray mine or
was sabotaged.

According to officials of the missing tanker's owner,
Marine Transport Lines of New York, sulphur, kept

in a liquid state, with 265-degree steel coils, was as safe as most cargoes. Regarding sabotage or hitting a mine, the possibility was so remote that it was dismissed.

A Coast Guard officer said that if sulphur should come in contact with sea water, the ship "would go up like an atom bomb." Expert witnesses, including a chemist associated with the Texas Sulphur Company, shipper of the cargo, testified that scientists did not believe that molten sulphur could explode, even if sea water entered the tanks.

### 3. It broke in half

Maybe because of the storm she broke in half or was capsized by a great wave.

Seamen familiar with the missing tanker testified that a ship like the *Queen* just didn't go down very fast, at least so fast that she wouldn't be able to get off an emergency radio message. If she was being battered badly enough to break up, or the seas were so rough she could be capsized, the captain surely would have sent out a distress signal. The *Queen* carried two high-frequency radio transmitters with emergency batteries, and she also had a radio telephone.

Several ships of the *Marine Sulphur Queen*'s class had cracked and split. But no evidence was developed to explain how this ship, even if she had split in half, could go down so quickly as to leave no trace.

Hundreds of the T-2-type tankers were built on a World War II design and did valiant service in the war. In the nature of such production-line ship construction, there were bugs. Quite a few broke in two, ten to be exact, but in all cases the halves, or at least one half, remained afloat. Most of the pieces were salvaged.

Officials of the ship line announced that another sulphur-ship was on order, a converted ship that would use the stern of a T-2 that had been cut in two.

## 4. It exploded from reaction of its own cargo

Witnesses told of a series of minor fires which surrounded the special tanks carrying the hot sulphur. They said these fires appeared to be from gases, and one likened them to burning cognac around Christmas pudding, in that they flared up and then were quickly spent.

An expert on explosives for the Department of the Interior's Bureau of Mines testified that gases formed by impurities in sulphur might have exploded. However, such an explosion probably would have been moderate because of escape vents.

All evidence presented only added to the mystery. Even though some items were discovered, the question of what happened to the 39 bodies of the crew still remained. Why were no lifeboats, oil slick, or floating sulphur found? Why was no distress message sent?

On Monday, May 27, 1963, the special Coast Guard Board of Inquiry, headed by Rear Admiral James D. Craik, ended. The report read, "No final conclusions as to the exact cause of the disappearance of the tanker could be offered." The S.S. *Marine Sulphur Queen* and her entire crew must be presumed lost. The admiral called the inquiry one of the longest in recent years, but without the satisfaction of reaching a concrete conclusion.

With those words, the *Marine Sulphur Queen* was written off as just one more unsolved mystery in the "Limbo of the Lost."

# LLOYD'S REGISTER OF SHIPPING

### 71, Fenchurch Street, London, E.C.3

*Telegraphic | Inland: Committee, London, Telex*
*Address | Overseas: Committee, London, E.C.3*

*Telephone: 01-709 9166*
*Telex No.: 34303*

Air Mail
Your Ref:  JWS/tkw                    2nd May 1969

*Please address further communications on this subject to THE SECRETARY and quote the following reference .*

**Statistics**

Dear Sir,

With reference to previous correspondence, and your letter of the 22nd April in particular, I have made a "dummy run" investigating within the perameters of your enquiry from both ends of the time span. The basis of our interpretation of your requirements is the category of loss we call "Missing". During the period 1962 to 1967 inclusive, only one ship, the former T-2 tanker the "MARINE SULPHUR QUEEN", flying the American flag of 7,240 tons gross was posted as missing in in this area. She had been converted to a molten sulphur carrier, with which she was loaded at the time, and was on her way from Beaumont to Norfolk, Virginia, when she disappeared in approximately latitude 26' 40° North longtitude 88' 0° West on the 3rd February 1963. I remember this case well because of the dangerous constituency of the cargo and volatile gas given off (Hydrogen Sulphide). Doubtless you can find more from the government enquiry which was made into this case for there was considerable loss of life.

I investigated the years 1890 to 1893 inclusive and discovered forty seven cases of ships missing.

The complete crew list of the missing vessel is as follows:

James V. Fanning, Master—Beaumont, Tex.
George E. Watson, Chief Mate—Galveston, Tex.
Henry P. Hall, 2nd Mate—Beaumont, Tex.
Frank J. Cunningham, 3rd Mate—Beaumont, Tex.
George E. Sloat, Radio Officer—Baltimore, Md.
Leon B. Clauser, Chief Engineer—Beaumont, Tex.
John L. Denton, 1st Asst. Engineer—Friendswood, Tex.
A. R. Van Sickle, 2nd Asst. Engineer—Baltimore, Md.
E. W. Schneeberger, 3rd Asst. Engineer—Beaumont, Tex.
Adam Martin, Jr., 3rd Asst. Engineer—Austin, Tex.
Evans Phillips, Bosun—Tampa, Fla.
Ceburn R. Cole, DM/AB—Lake Charles, La.
Jack R. Schindler, AB—Seattle, Wash.
Fred A. Bodden, AB—Philadelphia, Pa.
Everett E. Arnold, AB—Memphis, Tenn.
Willie T. Manuel, AB—Ville Platte, La.
James Mck. Bodden, AB—Tampa, Fla.
Nelaton E. Devine, AB—Port Arthur, Tex.
John M. Nieznajski, OS—Gary, Ind.
Clarence Mcguire, OS—Bronsen, Tex.
James Phillips, OS—Port Arthur, Tex.
Jesse I. Vicera, Pumpman—Linden, N.J.
Alejandro Valdez, Oiler—Port Arthur, Tex.
John C. Ardoin, Oiler—Beaumont, Tex.
John Elmer Grice, Oiler—Daytona Beach, Fla.
Henry Clark, FWT—Jersey City, N.J.
Alphan Tate, FWT—Philadelphia, Pa.
Leroy Courville, FWT—Groves, Tex.
John Husch, Jr., Wiper—Akron, Ohio
Aaron Heard, Wiper—Norfolk, Va.
Juan Santos, Wiper—Newark, N.J.
Charles L. Dorsey, Chief Steward—Bronx, N.Y.
Vincent Thompson, Chief Cook—Baltimore, Md.
Cornelius Smith, 2nd Cook & Baker—Port Arthur, Tex.
Hugh D. Hunter, Galleyman—Chapel Hill, N.C.
Walter Pleasant, Messman—Port Arthur, Tex.
Wesley Fontenot, Messman—Mamou, La.
Robert E. Harold, Utilityman—Norfolk, Va.
Leroy B. Green, Utilityman—Rahway, N.J.

# M/V *Southern Cities* Lost in Gulf, Saturday, October 29, 1966

## Missing crew members: 6

At approximately 11:45 on the night of October 29, 1966, the 85-gross-ton, 67-foot tugboat M/V *Southern Cities* departed Freeport, Texas. She was bound for Tuxpan, Mexico, with 6 persons on board and a 210-foot loaded barge in tow astern on a hawser. This was her fifth voyage since July 25, when a verbal contract with Bludworth Marine Equipment Company, Houston, Texas, and the *Southern Cities'* owner, F. W. Towing Company, Inc., Bella Chasse, Louisiana, was initiated. The agreement called for the towing of the 1,013 gross-ton, seagoing bulk-cargo barge, number B-1800, between Freeport and Tuxpan.

Three days after setting out on her last voyage the *Southern Cities'* owner received a report from the tug's master stating that she was 95 miles south of Port Isabel, Texas—43 miles offshore and 230 miles to go. She was making six knots, the weather was fine, no problems were being experienced, and it was estimated she would arrive at Tuxpan on the morning of Thursday, November 3. It was further acknowledged that another report would be made the next morning. It was to be relayed through the M/V *Texan,* another tug located approximately 18 miles southeast of Tuxpan attending a Mexican government drilling barge.

On the morning of November 2, the *Southern Cities'* owner was notified that no report had been received. The following morning the company was again advised that no report had been received from their vessel. Shortly thereafter, at 8:34, the U.S. Coast Guard Rescue Coordination Center in New Orleans was contacted by the *Southern Cities* owner and a formal request for aircraft assistance in locating and establishing communications with the missing tug was initiated.

An air search of 8,400 square miles was made along the estimated tow route north of Tuxpan. When nothing was located an intensive hunt began, covering a line from a position 15 miles off Vera Cruz, Mexico, to Tuxpan. In addition, an area from Tuxpan to latitude 24° north, about 15 to 40 miles off the coast, was scanned by air and surface craft.

At 8:33 on the morning of November 5, barge B-1800 was located by search craft drifting 105 miles north of Tuxpan. The barge was undamaged, there was no mark of recently caused indentations, and her cargo of bulk soda ash, caustic, and amines contained in drums of various sizes, was intact. The 600-foot-long, 8-inch polypropylene towline was still made fast to the barge, and the chafing chain and hawser, which were normally secured to the towing bitt of the *Southern Cities,* were also intact.

At 2:05 in the afternoon of the same day that the barge was located, one adult cork life preserver was recovered 120 miles from Tampico, Mexico. In a near vicinity, two broken sections of a name board were recovered, which when fitted together bore the name "uthern Cities." Also recovered was a 24-foot length of unraveled tow line. Several days later, a ring life buoy was found approximately 15 miles south of the Port Isabel, Texas, jetties.

As in the disappearance of the *Marine Sulphur Queen*

the few bits of debris only tended to confuse rather than to assist the investigators. Negligence due to lack of safety precautions must be eliminated. She was given a thorough drydock check and overhaul at Houston a month and a half before her disappearance. The missing tug was equipped with a 20-man balsa life float, 5 30-inch ring life buoys, 12 life preservers, and 9 fire extinguishers. The *Southern Cities* was similar to the various designs of the ST-type (small tug) harbor tugs built for the Army Transportation Corps during World War II. At the time of her disappearance, her market value was estimated at $30,000, with a replacement cost of approximately $125,000.

The search was officially terminated as of dusk November 8. The number of aircraft flights or sorties during the hunt was listed as 43, totaling 253.3 hours and covering 84,600 square miles. The last known reported position of the *Southern Cities* was used as the starting point in the search.

On November 28, 1966, the Department of Transportation, United States Coast Guard, Marine Board of Investigation released a report which I quote in part:

In the absence of survivors or physical remains of the ship, the exact cause of the loss of the M/V *Southern Cities* cannot be determined. . . . Although there is no evidence indicating a failure of the vessel's radio equipment, the failure of the vessel to transmit a distress message appears to justify the conclusion that the loss of the vessel may have occurred so rapidly as to preclude the transmission of such a message. . . . The six men are presumed dead as a result of the casualty. There has been no trace of them since the sinking. There is no probability that the vessel or any of the six persons on board will be recovered. . . .

It is further concluded that there is no evidence of negligence, misconduct or foul play on the part of any of the crew members. There is no evidence of violation of laws or regulations enforced by the U.S. Coast Guard. It is finally concluded that there is no evidence that any personnel of the Coast Guard or any other government agency or any other person contributed to the casualty. It is recommended that the case be closed and no further action be taken.

Other than the few items found, no other debris or gear belonging to the M/V *Southern Cities* or her crew was ever located. It was as though she just foundered into the "Limbo of the Lost."

A list of the six missing crew members is as follows:

Grady A. Reynolds, 27, Master—New Orleans, La.
Victor L. Benton, 41, Mate—Omega, Ga.
Clyde Wesley Sparkman, 45, Engineer—Houston, Tex.
George R. Johnson, 38, Deckhand—Jacksonville, Fla.
Buddy Lee, 45, Deckhand—Perry, Fla.
Thomas E. Rollins, 40, Deckhand—Perry, Fla.

All of the above persons were employed by F. W. Towing Company, Inc., owners of the M/V *Southern Cities*.

**DEPARTMENT OF TRANSPORTATION**
**UNITED STATES COAST GUARD**

Address reply to:

5943
M/V SOUTHERN CITIES
14, 28 November 1966

From: Marine Board of Investigation
To: Commandant (MVI)

Subj: M/V SOUTHERN CITIES, O.N. 241635; Disappearance in the Gulf of Mexico on or about 1 November 1966, with loss of life

Findings of Fact:

1. At approximately 2345, +6 zone time, on 29 October 1966, the M/V SOUTHERN CITIES, O.N. 241635, departed Freeport, Texas, bound for Tuxpan, Mexico, with six (6) persons on board and with loaded barge B-1800, O.N. 293266, in tow astern on a hawser. At approximately 0630 on 1 November 1966, the vessel reported her position as Latitude 24°-30' North and Longitude 96°-40' West. No further communication was received from the M/V SOUTHERN CITIES. At 0833, on 5 November 1966, barge B-1800 was located drifting in position Latitude 22°-45' North and Longitude 97°-15' West. The M/V SOUTHERN CITIES was never found, nor were any of the six (6) persons that were on board.

2. The M/V SOUTHERN CITIES, O.N. 241635, was a welded steel single screw diesel propelled towing vessel built in 1942 at Walker Shipyard, Pascagoula, Mississippi, for the Southern Tug & Barge Company of New Orleans, Louisiana. She was similar to the various designs of the ST type harbor tugs built for the Army Transportation Corps during World War II. The M/V SOUTHERN CITIES, of New Orleans, Louisiana, was powered by a 400 brake horsepower, 6 cylinder, 4 cycle air started, direct reversible Atlas Imperial diesel engine, engineroom controlled. Her registered dimensions were 67 feet in length, 19.1 feet in breadth and 7.7 feet in depth. She was of 85 gross tons and 57 net tons. The vessel was owned and operated by F. W. Towing Company, Inc., of Box 232 E, Belle Chasse, Louisiana. Frank Wyman, of the above address, was President. The Master was Grady A. Reynolds, of 701 Forstall Street, New Orleans, Louisiana, License 36372, operator of mechanically propelled vessels of 100 gross tons or less on waters other than ocean or coastwise. The vessel was purchased from Arkansas Navigation Company, Inc., of Box 207, Osceola, Arkansas, in February 1966. The SOUTHERN CITIES was not subject to inspection by the U. S. Coast Guard, being under 300 gross tons, and had never been in class with a Classification Society. Also, the persons on board were not required to be licensed or certificated. No stability data of the SOUTHERN CITIES could be obtained.

# IV

## Ghost Ships
## and Sea Serpents

## The Brigantine *Mary Celeste*
## Found Abandoned
## Wednesday, December 4, 1872

On the afternoon of Wednesday, December 4, 1872, the *Dei Gratia*, ("By Grace of God"), a British brigantine, out of New York since November 15, was sailing between the Azores and Portugal, heading for Gibraltar. At one o'clock the ship's captain, David R. Morehouse, sighted a vessel, also a brigantine, *Mary Celeste*, seemingly in trouble about four or five miles off. Her sails were torn, she was listing badly, no sailors were on deck nor anyone at her wheel, yet she was not displaying a distress signal.

Captain Morehouse ordered three men to board her and render assistance if needed. About one hour later the bewildered sailors reported that no one was aboard, alive or dead. It was as though the entire ship's company of ten, including the ship's cat, had vanished into thin air.

There were no boats on board, all hatch doors were wide open, the wheel was operating freely, and the compass stand was knocked out of place and the compass broken. Chronometer, sextant, ship's register, and navigation book were nowhere to be found. However, the ship's log, showing regular daily entries, was located in the mate's cabin. The working log, a slate kept by the mate, showed that at eight o'clock on the morning of Monday, November 25, the *Mary Celeste* passed six miles off the eastern tip of Saint Mary's Island (Santa Marie, the Azores), about 800 miles from Portugal.

Her cargo of 1,701 barrels of alcohol, worth about $42,000, was intact in the hold, covered by 3 to 4 feet of seawater. The galley was in perfect order and the dinner table was clean, indicating that the crew was not about to eat. No wine, beer, or spirits were allowed on board as Captain Benjamin Spooner Briggs was a firm believer in temperance.

In the crew's quarters, the seamen's personal belongings were untouched. Their lockers contained various items of value, including money and the one thing no mariner would ever leave behind, his pipe. In the captain's cabin, the berth was unmade, and on the floor were his boots and raincoat.

All the evidence pointed to one conclusion: the vessel had been abandoned hastily, sometime between 8:00 A.M. and noon.

As Captain Morehouse studied the situation, I am sure he could not help but think back to the evening of November 5, two days before the *Mary Celeste* set sail for Genoa. He probably recalled having had dinner with the 37-year-old captain, Ben Briggs, and his wife Sarah in New York. It was the custom in those days for the wife and children of the ship's master to accompany him to sea.

Captain Morehouse discussed the matter of the *Mary Celeste* with his first mate, who wanted to claim the derelict for the salvage money. After a lengthy discussion the captain agreed, but explained that they had 600 miles to go before reaching the nearest port of Gibraltar, and he could spare only two seamen besides the mate as a crew. Knowing fully the dangers involved, they set off, sailing side by side.

Luckily the weather remained calm for six days. Then on December 11, as they sighted Cape Spartel, Morocco, a vicious storm of high winds and pelting rain began. During the night the two ships lost sight of one another.

On December 12 the *Dei Gratia* reached Gibraltar, and the next day the *Mary Celeste* arrived. The mate, with his crew of two, certainly earned consideration for a generous salvage reward, the hard way. But the battle for the spoils was just beginning.

A salvage hearing began on December 18 and lasted until March 14, 1873. Captain Morehouse and his crew were accused of foul play, conspiracy, and murder. When all was said and done, the owners and crew of the *Dei Gratia* were cleared and divided $8,300, certainly a poor reward for their deed.

The story really began ten years earlier, in 1861. The *Mary Celeste,* then named *Amazon,* was launched at Spencer Island shipyard, Nova Scotia. She was registered in a nearby port on June 10. The first captain was a Robert McLellan, who died of pneumonia nine days after the ship's registration.

The second skipper was Captain John (Jack) Nutting Parker. He took over and sailed to Portland, Maine. On the return voyage the *Amazon* crashed into a fishing boat. Both craft were extensively damaged. After repairs, the jinx ship set sail for London, then to France, but in the straits of Dover she ran into a brig, sending it to the bottom.

On November 9, 1867, the *Amazon* ran ashore at Cow Bay, Cape Breton Island. The situation appeared hopeless, so she was abandoned to salvage. To make matters worse, the *Amazon* was not covered by insurance and was sold for a small sum, just as she lay.

Alexander McBean purchased the craft, pulled it off the shore, and placed her back in service. Twelve months later, in November 1868, without an explanation, McBean sold the *Amazon* at auction in New York.

The new owner changed her registry from British to American and also changed her name to *Mary Celeste*. She sailed the seas for about a year, but the new owner had no luck with her. Subsequently, she was seized in New York and sold for the debt.

From 1866 to 1872 a variety of minor catastrophes befell the owners and captains of the *Mary Celeste*. This takes us back to the beginning of the story, but it doesn't end here.

For 12 years after her abandonment in 1872, the *Mary Celeste* sailed the oceans. In December 1884, Captain Gilman C. Parker of Winthrop, Massachusetts, took her to sea from Boston and deliberately smashed the brigantine into a coral reef near Haiti in the West Indies, for insurance money.

The plot was discovered and Captain Parker was tried, but on a legal technicality was found innocent and released. Captain Parker didn't win, for he was never allowed to sail as a sea captain again. In July 1891 he died, a broken man.

*Mary Celeste* will always rank as the number-one derelict jinx ship that voyaged into the unknown seas of the "Limbo of the Lost."

# What Happened to the Crews of Colite and *Rubicon*?

*Gloria Colite, February 3, 1940*

The 125-foot Schooner *Gloria Colite* of St. Vincent, British West Indies, was sighted on the afternoon of February 3, 1940, apparently abandoned. Her reported position was about 150 miles south of Mobile, Alabama.

The U.S. Coast Guard cutter *Cardigan,* which was operating in the Gulf, was sent to the scene. She took the derelict in tow, and the cutter's captain radioed that the vessel's decks were a mass of wreckage, her deck housing smashed, and her foresails were set, but badly torn. Her mainsail, rigging, and steering were gone, and no trace of her crew was found. No clues were uncovered that could shed any light as to why her crew left the schooner at the mercy of the sea.

On the afternoon of February 5, the *Cardigan* arrived at Mobile with her charge. A full investigation was launched, but without success.

*Rubicon, October 22, 1944*

Another noted maritime abandonment mystery occurred on October 22, 1944. This time a Cuban cargo ship, the *Rubicon,* of approximately 90 gross tons, was found adrift and apparently abandoned in the Gulf stream 30 miles southeast of Key Largo, Florida.

A Navy blimp spotted the ship and notified the Coast Guard at Miami. Two boats were dispatched to investigate, but when they arrived at the scene they found the derelict ship *Rubicon* had already been taken in tow under salvage law by the *Nirvana,* a banana boat of United States registry.

Eighteen hours later, all four vessels put into the quarantine dock at Miami, and a full investigation was begun. It was noted that the only living creature on board the *Rubicon* was a half-starved dog. The life-boats were gone and a broken hawser was hanging over the bow; otherwise she was apparently in excellent shape. The last entry in the ship's log was dated September 26, when she apparently put into Havana harbor. This information only added to the mystery, because the air distance from Havana to the spot where she was picked up is estimated at some 200 miles. There seems to be no logical explanation for the obvious abandonment.

To this day, nobody anywhere has been able to say for sure what became of the crews of the *Gloria Colite* or the *Rubicon.* It appears they became just another unfortunate part of the maritime mystery surrounding the "Limbo of the Lost."

## The Disappearance of the British Training Ship *Atalanta*

In January 1880, Captain Francis Stirling, master of the British training ship *Atalanta,* set sail for the long voyage back to England from the sunny shores of Bermuda. He planned to arrive at Spithead about March 1 with his charge of over 300 young seamen trainees.

When the *Atalanta* was reported as two weeks over-due, the British Channel squadron and the dispatch vessel *Salamis* left Gibraltar in search of her.

A dispatch from Portsmouth, England, on April 26 read, "No news had been received in reference to the *Atalanta*." Even the most optimistic were beginning to lose heart.

One of the many search ships returned to England in May with the sad news that there was nothing to report and that most likely all those aboard the training ship were lost at sea forever.

The only hope now remaining was a desperate supposition that the *Atalanta* may have been driven far to the north. British Admiralty officials said they received 150 telegrams and 200 personal requests that the coasts of Greenland and Iceland be thoroughly searched.

First report came from the British Gunboat *Avon,* which sighted masses of wreckage from an unidentified vessel off the Azores, close to the usual route of training ships.

Nothing was discovered in the waters bearing the training ship's name, and after a further search of the area proved fruitless, Admiral Hood's British channel squadron headed to Bantry Bay. He expected to arrive on or about May 8 for further orders.

In April 1880, a report was circulated that the steamer *Tamar,* from the West Indies, passed a capsized, copper-bottomed ship.

Conjecture associated this report with the *Atalanta,* but the good captain of the *Tamar* contradicted the whole story, saying he saw no such vessel.

On April 28 the British Admiralty received word that a bottle had been picked up at the junction of the

Weaver and Mersey rivers containing a paper inscribed, "H.M.S. *Atalanta*, 16th March—fearful hurricane; dismasted; going down fast."

After an investigation a statement was released saying, the message was undoubtedly a discreditable hoax.

On April 20, Her Majesty's store ship *Wye* left Gibraltar to search the area of Vigo Bay, Spain, where portions of a wrecked vessel washed ashore.

She arrived at Plymouth, England on April 29 and reported that nothing new had been discovered relating to the fate of the missing training ship.

On June 2, the captain of a vessel which had arrived at Queenstown from Demerara reported that on April 30, in latitude 30° north, longitude 60° west, he passed a raft. It was apparently made on board a man-of-war or a first class steamer, because it was bolted together, not lashed. Two days later, he said he saw several corpses dressed in white. Rumor had it that another vessel saw the same raft and two corpses dressed as naval seamen.

Speculation was that the rafts and the missing training ship were related, but it was never proved.

On June 15, a special dispatch from Rockport, Massachusetts, read, "Captain Edward Millett picked up a bottle floating in the water about a mile off Boston Harbor, containing a leaf from a pocket memorandum-book, on which was written, with great apparent haste, the following: 'April 17, 1880: Training ship *Atalanta*. We are sinking in longitude 27°, latitude 32°, any person finding this note will please advertise in the daily paper, John L. Hutchings, distress'."

On June 21, some children playing on the beach at Cow Bay, Nova Scotia, picked up a piece of barrel stave on which the following was written with a lead pencil: "*Atalanta* going down, April 12, 1880; no hope; send this to Mrs. Mary White, Piers, Sussex. James White."

The piece of wood appeared to have been in the water about two months. The place where it was picked up is about twelve miles east of Halifax and opens directly into the Atlantic Ocean.

On August 7, the admiralty office received a telegram from St. John, New Brunswick, reporting the finding of the *Atalanta*'s figurehead. The dispatch was described as being of the sensational type, saying that the vessel had been in collision with an iceberg.

Investigation revealed that no figurehead had been found and that no such vessel entered the port at St. John. The whole story was therefore listed as a fabrication.

The report of the investigating committee on the loss of the British training ship *Atalanta* was published on December 29, 1880, and stated no reliable trace had been found. The committee said they considered the *Atalanta* a very stable ship, except at the large angles of the heel, and that the alterations in her rig only tended to increase her safety. The committee spoke favorably of her officers and crew, and pointed out that at the time of her loss exceptional storms proved fatal to a number of merchant vessels. The only exception was that survivors or debris in the other cases were always found.

Experts agreed that the *Atalanta* must have encountered stormy weather, but so did scores of other vessels that crossed the Atlantic Ocean at the same time; yet the other vessels met with no mishaps other than slight delays. They pointed out that a British naval vessel was much safer than a merchant ship.

If military men could not manage a well-equipped sailing vessel in a storm, what would happen to them if they found themselves in mid-ocean on board a disabled ironclad?

The only sure fact is that the staunch and well-fitted *Atalanta* sailed into the port of the "Limbo of the Lost" and was never afterward heard from.

## The Flying Dutchman, Banshee Ship of Doom

While talking to groups about the mystery of the "Limbo of the Lost," invariably someone asks about the *Flying Dutchman.* Therefore I have included this section.

As far as I can determine, the legend began in the mid-1600s. Superstitious seamen told tales about a Captain Vanderdecken from Holland who, during a violent storm, was trying to round the Cape of Good Hope. The crew and passengers, fearing for their lives, requested that Captain Vanderdecken turn back, for it was certain that everyone aboard would surely be lost at sea. The phantom sea captain, puffing on his huge pipe, laughed at their request and at the top of his voice began singing irreverent songs. As he cursed, his masts snapped under the force of the winds and his sails carried away. The people again begged him for their lives, but to no avail.

When his first mate tried to force him to take the ship to shelter in a nearby bay, the mad captain flung him overboard. Upon seeing this, the crew and passengers began to pray for help. As if in answer to their prayers, an angel, or maybe even God himself, appeared before the captain.

With many variations, the conversation was said to go something like this:

VISION: You are very stubborn.

CAPTAIN: And you're a rascal. I do not want a peaceful voyage. I will round the Cape if it takes me to Judgment Day. I ask nothing of you, so get clear before I blow out your brains.

When the Vision did not move, Captain Vanderdecken picked up his pistol and fired. Bewildered because the bullet did not seem to interfere with the Vision, he tried to strike it with his fist, but his arm became paralyzed. He cursed and blasphemed and called God a variety of impious names.

VISION: From this time on you are accursed, condemned to sail upon the high seas without rest or anchorage or port of any kind. You shall have neither beer nor tobacco, and vinegar shall be your drink and red-hot coal your meat. It will always be your watch, and you will not be able to sleep, for when you close your eyes, a sword shall pierce your body. Since it has been your sport to torment sailors, torment them you will. You will be known as the evil spirit of the sea. You will cross all latitudes of the southern seas without relief or rest, and misfortune will befall all who cross your bow. On Judgment Day you will be claimed by the devil.

Captain Vanderdecken's answer to all that was simply, "A fig for the devil." With that last comment the "Vision," crew, and passengers vanished. Damned and alone except for his demon cabinboy, he sailed the seas plaguing mariners.

Legend has it that whenever the *Flying Dutchman* was seen, catastrophe occurred, such as:

A false course set, then shipwreck.

Wine turned sour and all food became beans.

Sometimes the *Flying Dutchman* would send letters to the captain of a ship meeting her; if read, the ship was lost.

If a boat was sent alongside the phantom ship, it would disappear with all hands.

The *Flying Dutchman* would on occasion change the appearance of his ship so that it was not readily recognized. It was said that the *Flying Dutchman* gathered a collection of seamen as cursed as himself; all criminals, pirates, and cowards.

For the mariner of those days and even until the late 1800s, the story was told and believed by many. I am the first to admit that anything is possible at sea, but I must also add, it is highly unlikely that there ever was a *Flying Dutchman*.


## Do Sea Serpents Really Exist?

The stories about gigantic sea monsters may not be just simply tales told by superstitious mariners, after all. Because of recent discoveries, many scientists have very good reasons for believing in the existence of giant sea serpents.

Dr. Robert J. Menzies, University of Southern California marine biologist, was credited with the discovery of the Neopilina, a very small sea animal that was believed extinct for over 300 million years.

Dr. Anton F. Bruun, lecturer on oceanology at the University of Copenhagen, Denmark, reported that on a night in February 1930, off the southwest coast of Africa, between the Cape of Good Hope and the small island of St. Helena, he captured, in a net, a six-foot-long Leptocephalus (baby eel). He said it had a small pointed head, with long fangs in its jaws, and seemed to be a typical larval eel in all respects except for its gigantic size. If the same ratio of growth that was known of other members of the eel family were applied, the parents of the 2 yard eel would be at least a length of 30 to 50 feet.

Professor L. R. Richardson of Victoria University in New Zealand reported finding an immature larval eel three feet long. The baby eel had a reptilian head, large sharp teeth, and well developed eyes. It was believed to be a different species than Dr. Bruun's discovery; however the projected size of its parents would also be very large, possibly about 30 feet.

Captain Peter M'Quhae, in command of the British frigate *Daedalus*, was sailing in the Atlantic between the Cape of Good Hope and St. Helena on August 6, 1848. At 5:00 P.M. his crew called his attention to an enormous, 60-foot-long sea serpent. He reported that the monster passed rapidly, but so close, as he put it, "that had it been a man of my acquaintance, I should have easily recognized his features with the naked eye." The creature's southwest course never deviated and it held a pace of approximately 12 to 15 miles per hour.

Captain M'Quhae said, "The diameter of the Serpent was about 15 or 16 inches behind the head, which was, without any doubt, that of a snake. Its color was dark brown, with yellowish white about the throat. It had no fins, but something like the mane of a horse, or rather, a bunch of seaweed, washed about its back."

The Master of the American brig *Daphne* in South Atlantic waters on September 20, 1848 reported seeing "a most extraordinary animal about 100 feet long. . . . The appearance of a huge serpent or snake."

When the serpent was a distance of only 40 yards from the *Daphne,* they fired a deck gun loaded with spikes at it. The monster reared its head in the air and plunged violently, foaming and lashing the water. As the ship approached, the brute, although wounded, raced off at 15 or 16 knots.

Two British Zoologists, Michael J. Nicoll and E. G. B. Meade-Waldo, were aboard the yacht *Valhalla,* off Parahiba, Brazil, on December 7, 1905. At about 10:00 A.M. the two zoologists saw a large fin or frill, somewhat crinkled at the edge, sticking out of the water.

The monster had a great turtlelike head; the neck was about as thick as a man's body, and it rose about seven or eight feet out of the water. The color of the head and neck, which moved from side to side in a strange manner, was dark seaweed-brown above and whitish below. The yacht quickly sailed away from the strange creature, which was traveling very slowly.

The captain of the Grace Liner, *Santa Clara* reported that he and his crew sighted a snakelike sea serpent at 11:55 A.M. on December 30, 1947, while they were steaming southwest through the calm waters about 120 miles east of Cape Lookout, North Carolina.

The dark brown, slick and smooth monster was first spotted 30 feet off the starboard bow. As it approached abeam of the bridge, the witnesses noticed blood staining an area 30 to 40 square feet around the creature. The visible part of its body was about 35 feet long. Presumably the stem of their ship had cut the snake-like monster in two. No fins, hair, or protuberances on the head, neck, or visible parts of the body could be seen.

From the time the serpent was first sighted until it vanished in the distance, it thrashed about as though in agony.

## The Loch Ness Monster

Loch Ness, the largest mass of fresh water in the United Kingdom, is said to be inhabited by an aquatic monster, accounts of which have been publicized since the early 1930s.

The quiet 700 square miles of lake stretches southwest and northeast 24 miles, has a uniform width of about a mile, and depths of 754 feet. Nestled in Scotland's bonnie highlands, six miles from Inverness, the famous ice-free lake is fed by several large rivers known for salmon fishing.

The unidentified swimming object, affectionately named "Nessie" by its seekers, is not known to be a "he" or a "she." Many people scoff at its existence, while others are firm believers. Speculations on what it might actually be range from a submarine to some sort of curiosity left over from prehistoric days.

Many scientists believe there is little doubt that something is in the loch. In fact, they think there may be a whole clan of somethings breeding in the murky water of the lake.

A movie film taken in 1959 has been analyzed by the British Joint Air Reconnaissance Intelligence Center (JARIC). The JARIC experts are recognized as among the world's best photographic interpreters. They took measurements on every frame of the film, taking into consideration light conditions, reflections, the angle of the object, and the position of the camera.

Their conclusions? The object was not a surface vessel, nor was it a submarine; "leaving the conclusion that it probably is an animate object." It was moving along at about ten miles an hour. By a series of measurements and reasonings, the experts deduced that the object, though most of it was beneath the surface, was approximately 92 feet long, not less than 6 feet wide, and not more than 5 feet high.

That description would seem to fit "sea serpent" rather well. British Air Defense Minister Lord Shackleton commented on the JARIC finding: "I have always disbelieved in the Loch Ness Monster, but now I am even more mystified. I find it difficult to discount the finding of this report."

Up to 500 members of the Phenomena Investigation Bureau, Limited, take turns camping out on the shores of the loch every year, from the middle of March to the middle of October.

Armed with field-glasses, long pads, and 35-millimeter movie cameras with telephoto lenses, they keep a record of anything that moves on the lake. According to observers' reports, "Nessie" has been sighted many times. But a clear, well-focused, unmistakable picture has yet to be taken at least as of this writing.

The sightings haven't all been in recent years, either. Local legends go back centuries, including one involving Saint Columba, the Abbot of Iona. He made the first recorded sighting in A.D. 565. According to the chronicles, "the Holy man gave a great shout and commanded the beast to go back into the depths from which he came." The monster obligingly did so, and ever since, one of its often reported characteristics has been a fear of noise.

A retired British Navy officer, Lieutenant Commander Francis Flint of Burgess Hill, Sussex, said he knows it's actually there because he hit it in 1943 and damaged his motor launch. He said he didn't actually see the monster, but he didn't see anything else that could have caused the jolting impact or damage to his launch, either.

Attempts to locate "Nessie" by sonar have failed in the past because of the echoes from the steep underwater walls of the loch. In the summer of 1968, a new kind of sonar was tried, developed by engineers at England's University of Birmingham. It uses a computer to screen out the confusing echoes, and during testing it found something large and moving in the depths of Loch Ness.

A favorite theory is that "Nessie" is a descendant of some big-bodied, long-necked reptiles (lizards or eels) called Plesiosaurs, which roamed the steamy world more than 100 million years ago. How the Plesiosaur survived the succession of ice ages since, isn't explained.

A less romantic theory is that the Loch Ness monster is a full-grown specimen of one of those giant eel larvae that oceanographers occasionally fish up from the ocean depths.

The British government still maintains an official disbelief in "Nessie," but for some unknown reason a law was placed on the books in 1934 officially protecting the nonexistent monster of Loch Ness from harm by hunters.

Whatever "Nessie" might be, the Scots have forbidden anyone from harming her. They say they would most vigorously oppose any attempt by anyone to touch one hair of its hide, that is supposing it has hair or for that matter, a hide.

# V

# Piracy on the High Seas

# The Strange Case of *Carol Deering*

One of the strangest mysteries of the "Limbo of the Lost" involved the 5-masted, 3,500-ton, American schooner, *Carol* [Carroll A.] *Deering* of Portland, Maine. She usually sailed the trade routes between her home port and Barbados, so it was not strange that in December 1920 she departed Portland for Rio de Janeiro with a general cargo.

The *Deering* arrived on schedule without incident, took on a new general cargo, and started out on a return voyage. She was cleared for Norfolk, Virginia, with a stop scheduled at Barbados. As had been the routine for many years, she arrived at the British West Indies port for further orders. When no change was received, she set sail for Norfolk.

On January 29, the schooner made contact with the Cape Lookout Lightship, North Carolina, asking that her managing owners, G. G. Deering Company of Portland, be notified that she had lost both anchors. The request was made by a man other than the *Deering*'s master, Captain Willis B. Wormwell. Otherwise, the schooner appeared to be in very good condition, sailing at a speed of about five nautical miles.

A short time later, a steamer, the name of which was not ascertained, was passing the lightship when the Master of the Light signaled the vessel to stop in order to take a message for forwarding. In spite of numerous attempts to attract the steamer's attention, no response was given.

Two days later, January 31, the *Carol Deering* was found washed ashore a few miles north of the lightship at Diamond Shoals. Her crew of 12 officers and men were nowhere to be found.

Officials from the nearest lifesaving station boarded her and reported finding evidence that indicated abandonment took place in a hurry, yet for no conceivable reason. They noted that her motor lifeboat and dory were gone, and most of the provisions, clothing, and supplies of the vessel had been removed. She was in good shape, her sails were fully set, and the general cargo seemed to be untouched.

Coast Guard vessels began the search for survivors by slipping in and out of coves and inlets along the North Carolina coast in hope of picking up some clue —a bit of wreckage or a note which might have been left by a member of the *Deering*'s crew. For 70 days the hunt was conducted, and yet not a trace of the crew or wreckage of her small boats had been discovered.

On April 11, 1921, Christopher Columbus Ray reported that he found a bottle containing a message near his home at Buxton Beach, North Carolina, near Cape Hatteras. The unsigned note was believed written by the *Carol Deering*'s mate, Engineer Henry Bates. The message read as follows: "Deering captured by oil-burning boat something like chaser, taking off everything, handcuffing crew. Crew hiding all over ship. No chance to make escape. Finder please notify headquarters of Deering."

On May 23, 1921, the Reverend Addison B. Lorimer, pastor of the Central Square Baptist Church of Portland, and Miss Lulu Wormwell, daughter of the *Deering*'s captain, sent a telegram to Senator Frederick Hale of Maine, asking for an appointment to see the Secretary of Commerce, Herbert Hoover. The telegram indicated that they had certain important facts relating to "piracy on the high seas."

The appointment was made, they went to Washington, and were seen by Secretary Hoover, Senator Hale, Secretary Hughes, and Commodore Reynolds of the Coast Guard Services. Reverend Lorimer and Miss Wormwell presented compiled evidence concering the disappearance of the *Deering*'s crew, including the message purporting to have been written by the ship's mate, as well as other information pertaining to several additional ships that had vanished within the period of one year.

The evidence seemed so conclusive that an investigation was started by five departments of the Washington government:

State Department—instructed its consular officers at ports throughout the world to be on the lookout for several missing vessels or members of the alleged kidnapped crew of the *Carol Deering*.

Treasury Department—through its Coast Guard and Lifesaving service, launched a gigantic search of the Atlantic coast of the United States and adjacent waters.

Navy Department—dispatched vessels to assist other agencies involved in the search.

105

Department of Commerce—through its Bureau of Navigation joined in to help the attempt to lift the veil of mystery.

Department of Justice—assigned some of its best agents to the case, for the government was working on the theory of "foul play" and that all of the incidents were possibly interrelated.

Government officials stated difficulty in believing that acts of piracy could have been committed in or near the territorial waters of the United States. But the circumstantial evidence pointed to the suspicion that all the mysterious happenings were brought about by persons willing to take the chance of committing old-time piratical crimes.

Perhaps the cause for the piracy was sincere sympathy for the Soviets or the merely greedy objective of disposing of pirated cargoes at extremely high prices to authorities of Soviet Russia. Possibly Soviet sympathizers had seized the vessels and sailed them directly to Russian ports.

On June 22, officials of the Department of Commerce were considering asking the military for planes to patrol the little-frequented stretches of coast near Cape Hatteras for some trace of the merchant vessels that mysteriously vanished there.

Government spokesmen stated that, if pirates had raided the ships and murdered or captured the crews, they would have had to leave some trace along the shores, either in the way of boats, wreckage, or dead bodies. It was pointed out that because the disappearances extended over a one-year period the raiding vessel or vessels would have needed a nearby base of operations. At no time did the officials declare positively that all of the missing ships were the victims of pirates or possibly Bolshevist sympathizers, but neither did they deny it.

Numerous others have disappeared over the years in mysterious circumstances.

I have compiled information about some of the vessels that disappeared off the coast of the United States during the period from April 1920 to April 1921. Four of them vanished in February 1921, and three of them sailed from Norfolk, Virginia, at about the same time.

The fate of the new wooden steamship, *William O'Brien,* a vessel of 3,143 tons, under charter of the France and Canada Steamship Company, had long been a topic of discussion in shipping circles. She left New York on April 14, 1920, bound for Rotterdam. The following day she put back to port. Her Captain said that he had experienced trouble with his crew, but would not elaborate.

On the tide of the next morning, the steamer made a fresh start. A few days later on Sunday, April 18, the steamer *Baltic* received a radio message from the *O'Brien* to the effect that she was 500 miles east of the Delaware River and needed assistance. Help was sent, but the freighter was never heard from again.

Three months later the mother of a member of the crew appeared at the office of the parent company with a postcard mailed in France and supposedly written in the hand of her son. It stated that he had been on a ship with Edsel Ford, son of Henry Ford. An investigation brought out the fact that the younger Ford was in Detroit at the time.

The Russian bark *Albyan* sailed from Norfolk on October 1, 1920. She was never heard from again and not the slightest trace of any wreckage was ever found.

A British schooner, *General Morne,* sailed from Lisbon for Newfoundland on October 19, 1920, and disappeared.

The Spanish steamer *Yute,* of 2,974 tons, sailed from Baltimore on November 14, 1920. On November 17 she was heard calling for help and gave her position as about 240 miles off the New Jersey coast, southeast of Cape May. Government vessels and other ships put out to her assistance, but were unable to find any trace.

The Norwegian bark *Flonine* left Hampton Roads on November 25, 1920, and disappeared.

An American steel steamer *Hewitt* of Portland, Maine, disappeared under equally mysterious circumstances. She sailed from Sabine, Texas, on January 20, 1921, bound for Boston and Portland with a cargo of sulphur. She was sighted about 250 miles north of Jupiter Inlet, Florida, but that was the last to be seen of her. Government authorities were unable to find any trace. Not a boat or a spar had come ashore or been picked up, and not a body of any member of her crew was found.

There was a remote possibility that the *Hewitt* might have been off Diamond Shoals about the same time the *Deering* went ashore. The Department of Commerce officials conjectured the *Hewitt* was still afloat and intact. Clarence A. Snider, secretary of the Union Sulphur Company, owners of the steamer said, "I do not believe that the *Hewitt* is still afloat nor intact.

We would have heard of her long before this. Anyway, we have collected the insurance on the craft." She was officially posted as missing on March 16, 1921.

The Italian steamer *Monte San Michele,* of 4,061 tons, left Portland with a cargo of grain for Genoa on February 2, 1921, and disappeared.

A British tank steamer, the *Ottawa* departed Port Lobos bound for Manchester, England. She stopped at Norfolk, Virginia, and sailed from there on February 2, 1921. The steamer was in radio communication on February 6 with the steamer *Dorlington Court.* Since then she has never been heard from.

A Brazilian steamer, the *Cabedello,* sailed from Norfolk on February 3, 1921, and disappeared.

The British schooner *Esperenza de Larrinaga* also sailed from Norfolk on February 3, 1921 and likewise disappeared.

The British schooner *Canadian Maid* sailed from Monte Cristo for New York on April 4, 1921, and disappeared.

## Theories of Piracy

Speculation as to what was going on at sea ran rampant. Everyone with the slightest bit of information had a theory.

In May 1921, prior to contacting Secretary Hoover,

Miss Wormwell told Harry C. Deering, of the firm that owned the derelict schooner, that she was going to ask for a government investigation relative to her theory of "piracy on the high seas." Mr. Deering replied that if an investigation was conducted he would have little faith in the outcome.

Captain William H. Merritt of South Portland, the *Deering*'s original commander said he would help Miss Wormwell, but he also was not impressed with the chances of a piracy investigation ever producing any concrete results.

Carroll A. Deering, for whom the schooner was named, remarked that twentieth-century pirates had excellent opportunity to work by purchasing naval craft being offered for sale. He said that under favorable circumstances, and because of the general belief that piracy was nonexistent, it could possibly be carried on undisturbed for a long time.

On June 21, members of the G. G. Deering Company stated they were not inclined to take seriously the theory that the *Carol Deering* was attacked by pirates, nor that Captain Wormwell and his crew were taken off and the vessel then allowed to sail along unmanaged.

Captain O. O. W. Parker, Marine Superintendent of the Shipping Board, put his feeling this way, "Piracy without a doubt still exists, and it has since the days of the Phoenicians."

Many ship owners said that it seemed unlikely that sea robbers could have preyed on 13 ships without the fact becoming known. In support of their contention, they pointed out that the use of on-board wireless radio apparatus was becoming almost universal. Also, the commerce lanes of the ocean were more crowded than ever before, and there was an international patrol which kept a close watch on things.

Many other ship owners, especially those familiar with sailing vessels and tramp steamers, gave credence to the opinion held by Washington officials that piracy was again being practiced, or that agents of Soviet Russia were seizing craft on the ocean.

Commodore Reynolds of the Coast Guard Services said that it was not likely that the men of the *Carol Deering* were taken to any South American or any accessible European port. In his opinion, the crew had not been landed anywhere. He suggested that there might have been a mutiny on an oil tanker, whose crew put the men of the *Deering* in irons and carried them away to parts unknown, or murdered them.

At this point I must add my own views. The theory of regular pirates cannot pass for more than the remotest of possibilities.

As for Red sympathizers acting as pirates for Soviet Russia, this certainly has been disproved by history alone. Let's assume Russian port pirates did exist. They would have been operating against world shipping, and their stolen cargoes would have had to be landed and sold. Doubtless there were men who would deal in stolen goods and not care how they had been obtained. But in those days, as today, shipping regulations throughout the world were against such traffic, making it too difficult and dangerous to be practical. So let's make the assumption that the pirates tried to carry their bounty back to Russia. I cannot believe that they were able to get through the Baltic or into the Black Sea undetected.

Another intriguing theory deals with the possibility of mutiny.

On June 21, 1921, Senator Hale of Maine, who first asked for a government investigation of the disappearance of the *Hewitt* and of the *Carol Deering*'s crew, advanced the theory that mutiny, not piracy, was the explanation of the sea mysteries. He declared that he did not take any stock in reports that a Russian or other submarine raider was in operation. He called attention to the statement in the unsigned message in the bottle, that the *Deering*'s crew had been taken off forcibly by another ship. He said, "I think it will be found to be a plain case of mutiny in at least one of the cases. Possibly the mutinous crew of one vessel boarded the other to get a navigator." It was a well-known fact that the *Deering*'s captain was an excellent and thoroughly reliable navigator.

Many shipping men, however, believed the disappearances of the vessels in question were caused by natural accidents rather than the activities of pirates or Bolshevist marauders. They insisted that the fate of some of the missing vessels was attributed to hitting mines, icebergs, derelicts and storms.

On June 23, 1921 weather bureau officials came forward with a theory that some of the ships that vanished had fallen victim to a series of unusually severe storms which were known to have swept certain areas of the Atlantic during the first weeks of February 1921. The weather bureau theorized that during a forbidding storm the *Deering*'s crew left their vessel in small boats and were lost. In contradiction, weather bureau files also contained reports from a number of ships which passed through the February disturbances and reached port safely.

On August 25, 1921, Lawrence Richey, special assistant to the Secretary of Commerce stated that the investigation by the five government departments was completed. Stories that the schooner *Carol Deering* had been captured by pirates of the Soviet Government of Russia were put to rest once and for all.

The report showed evidence that the mysterious note alleged to have been found in a bottle, telling the fantastic tale of capture by pirates, was a fake. Investigation proved that the bottle was of California manufacture and the paper was made in America. It was also determined that, because the bottle was of one pint capacity and had an extremely narrow neck, it would have been virtually impossible to get the paper out without first breaking the bottle.

Christopher Columbus Ray, who reported the discovery of the bottle, was interviewed by investigators of the government. His handwriting on the note and on letters he had sent to the customs officials at Norfolk, Virginia, were inspected. Government agents were satisfied that Ray had written both. Finally, after long hours of questioning, Ray admitted that the note did not come from the *Carol Deering*. He told a story about fishermen on the North Carolina coast having prepared it. Thus the bottle and note were finally accounted for.

Messages found in bottles thrown overboard from ships sinking or otherwise in desperate trouble have figured prominently in many an ocean tale. They have, of course, also played a part in some real tragedies of the sea, but the stories have been more numerous than the realities. It is also a fact that landsmen accept such tales more readily than experienced seafarers.

113

The five government departments handled the "note in the bottle" nicely. They sifted all available evidence in order to get to the bottom of the whole mystery, and yet in the end they had to admit failure.

What did happen to the *Carol Deering* and the other 12 vessels and their crews? Strange as it may seem, to this day nobody has ever been able to come up with an absolute answer. I believe the key to the secret lies within the "Limbo of the Lost."

## Blackbeard the Pirate

While researching the story surrounding the *Carol Deering*, I found myself wondering what kind of person a real pirate was. And as any mention of piracy usually brings to mind the most famous (and infamous) pirate of all—Blackbeard, I selected this most picturesque of all pirates to study.

His real name was Edward Teach. He was reputedly born in or near Bristol, England, and during his short lifetime he gained a reputation for being an accomplished sea captain. Although his career as an independent commander under the skull and crossbones lasted only about three years, from 1716 to 1718, he seemed to have performed sufficient curious and atrocious deeds to give him a place more prominent than that accorded to more gentlemanly rogues, who followed their chosen calling for half an ordinary lifetime. He was a most hardened villain, bold and daring to the last degree.

His name was due to his great remarkably black ugly beard, which like a frightful demon covered his whole

114

face. His gruesome whiskers were the pride of his life. We are told he trained and curled and nursed them until they were as luxuriant and almost as artificial in appearance as the great powdered wigs of the day. His appearance caused more terror on the high seas than any weapon.

Teach started his operations with St. Thomas as his base, but soon shifted to Nassau. From there he sailed for the coast of Virginia. On his way, he captured three vessels, among them a large French ship which he took for his own. Naming her the *Queen Anne's Revenge,* he armed the man-of-war with 40 large cannons and set out to accomplish, off the North American mainland, just what he had done among the islands.

Early in 1717, he ran aground off the coast of North Carolina and surrendered to Governor Charles Eden, a British official of the Colonies. Some historians say a partnership was formed between Teach and the unsavory governor, in which he was to give the governor part of the proceeds of the spoils from his raids. Blackbeard made his permanent headquarters at Edenton, North Carolina, where he operated with two large privateers and a small sloop which served as a tender.

During stormy nights, Blackbeard's men would tie a lantern to a horse's head and send the steed trotting up and down the coast to lure craft ashore, in the belief that the bobbing light, from seaward, would appear as that of a vessel in deep water. Because of these reported tales, this area of North Carolina has been officially named "Nag's Head."

Blackbeard not only had the chief rule, but the greatest control over his men of any pirate captain ever known. He would perpetrate the most abominable wickedness imaginable just to prove he was a man of blood and iron. Aware that no pirate captain was safe over his command unless he was known as the strongest hand on the vessel, he continually and deliberately practiced maltreatment of his men so that there might be no doubt as to who was master.

Many stories with many variations have been told of how he killed and wounded his own men simply to remind them that he was in authority. Teach used to invite a couple of his crew to drink with him in his cabin. While the bowl was passing, he would cock a pair of the 12 pistols he always carried, blow out the candle, and then fire under the table. A crew member who came out of this game with a shattered knee asked the meaning of it. "Damn you," snapped Blackbeard, "if I didn't kill one of you now and again, you'd forget who I am."

Blackbeard's authority owed more to his daily villainies than to the rooted belief of his followers that he was in league with, and protected by, the devil himself. One day he perpetrated an insane incident by turning the hold of his ship into what he was pleased to call "a little hell." The various accounts agree that he took some of his favorite followers below deck, and there proceeded to burn sulphur and brimstone, all the while drinking goblets of rum and howling as he imagined the devil might shriek in a happy environment. He was just testing the stay powers of his men, and when he proved he could remain in the sulphur-laden fumes longer than any of them, he proudly declared this was proof of his identity with the devil. With his half-crazed desire to be mistaken for the "evil one," Teach was a real, living, dime-novel character.

Blackbeard and his men lurked about the mouth of the James River and preyed on coastal shipping trade.

After a successful raid, he would run his small fleet back through the few and dangerous inlets, past the narrow sandbars that separate the Atlantic Ocean from the sounds that front on the North Carolina mainland.

In November 1718, Governor Alexander Spottiswood of Virginia organized an expedition against Blackbeard at the urgent requests of Virginia planters. Lieutenant Robert Maynard of the British Navy was chosen to lead a small convoy to trap and bring to justice one Edward Teach.

After careful naval planning, he engaged Blackbeard in combat. With his entire crew, Teach boarded the British man-of-war with a pistol in one hand and a cutlass in the other, but not until he had received 16 wounds by shot and steel did he finally die.

Lieutenant Maynard cut off the pirate's head and placed it on the bowspit of his vessel. With Teach's great black beard flowing in the sea breeze, the British vessel sailed into port to show everyone that the scourge of the merchants and planters was no more. A wealthy man obtained the skull and had it silvered for the purpose of making a drinking mug out of it.

Blackbeard left 14 wives, countless children, and buried treasure, which to this day has not been found.

# VI

The Mystery of the Sargasso Sea

Many people believe the answer to the strange disappearances within the "Limbo of the Lost" can be found hidden in the mysterious Sargasso Sea.

For more than four centuries it has been commonly believed that this area of the Atlantic Ocean was so thick with seaweed that ships could not penetrate it. But tales of floating masses of seaweed capable of stopping the progress of ships is quite fantastic.

The Sargasso Sea lies between the United States and the west coast of Africa. Its eastern boundary is near the Azores, the southern boundary somewhere near the West Indies. The western and northern borders shift considerably from season to season because of changing weather conditions.

Somewhat elliptical in shape, the Sargasso Sea can be located between 20° and 35° north latitude (parallels) and 30° and 70° west longitude (meridians).

This unusually quiet region is bounded by the clockwise currents of the Gulf Stream and North Atlantic current on the west and north; on the south by the equatorial drift; and on the east by a line which runs roughly along the submerged mountain ridge in the middle Atlantic. Because of ocean current variations and the shifting and meandering of the Gulf Stream, the borders of the area are not constant or sharply defined.

Precipitation in the region of the Sargasso Sea is low, evaporation is high, winds are light, causing a tropical haze, and the water is remarkably clear, warm, and extremely salty.

The noun *sargasso* comes from the Portuguese, *salgazo,* derived from a word which stands for tiny grapes. The genus Sargassum, sometimes called gulfweed, belongs to the brown algae family and bears small but prominent grape-shaped, berrylike bladders. The stems are brown, and the finely divided branchlets are covered with slender pointed leaves that vary from olive yellow to a delicate green.

Sargassum weed is picked up from island and mainland coasts to the southwest by the strong ocean currents, carried away from shore and floats in the mighty Gulf Stream, until deposited in a huge, quiet pool of seaweed.

Unlike any other part of the oceans of the world, this slowly drifting seaweed covers an area about equal in size to that of the entire United States, approximately two million square miles.

Rather than being continuous, the weeds lie in long parallel bands of various sizes, some stretching as far as the eye can see. In places, the mysterious sea of weeds is very thin, floating only on the surface, while in others it extends far below the surface.

The branchlets of the graceful Sargassum weed shelter hosts of swimming, floating, clinging creatures of strange shapes and habits. Shrimp, crabs, mollusks, and sea spiders, with spiny outgrowths colored to imitate the weed, hide among its leaflets. A remarkable nest building fish, the "marbled angler" of brown and yellow coloration, blends exactly with the gulfweed, and weaves gelatinous strings of egg clusters into the plant growth with its spiny handlike fins. Its nests contain thousands of eggs.

If a branch of the Sargassum weed is shaken, hundreds of many-colored denizens are seen rushing about in all directions, eager to return to the particular spot best adapted to conceal them.

On September 16, 1492, six weeks after Christopher Columbus sailed from Cadiz on his first epoch-making voyage, his ships began to notice the unusual plant life of the Sargasso Sea.

He reported in the journal of his first voyage encountering floating seaweed not far west of the Azores, and by the time he reached mid-ocean there was "such an abundance of weeds that the sea seemed to be covered with them; they came from the west."

Columbus took this for a sure sign that his little fleet of three ships was nearing land, but when they had sailed another week the wind died out, and the sea was so calm "that the sailors murmured, saying they had got into smooth water, where it would never blow to carry them back to Spain."

His sailors were naturally terrified, for they could not conceive of seaweed without rocks. So to assure them, records show, Columbus hove the lead line and found no bottom. Little did he realize that the ocean bottom lay nearly three miles below.

It was almost a month after Columbus saw the first Sargassum weed before he finally sighted the West Indies on October 14. He described the weed in great detail in his log, and implied that he had evidence of earlier voyages through the area. He said it was possible the Carthaginians reached the Sargasso as early as 530 B.C.

From antiquity down through the Middle Ages, this ocean region was called the "Sea of Darkness." The canny Phoenicians were perhaps the first tellers of the tale, for they frightened off prospective competitors in foreign commerce by dire stories of what awaited any foolhardy voyager beyond the Pillars of Hercules.

The Atlantic, they said, was a place of dreadful darkness, a muddy and a shallow sea, where great morasses of strange growth waited to twine their slimy tendrils about any ship that ventured there and hold it helpless prisoner forever.

The discovery of a large store of Phoenician coins on one of the Azores makes it seem quite certain that those daring navigators from African shores actually saw the Sargasso Sea and embroidered this foundation of fact with their own shrewd fancy.

For centuries later, explorers brought back further tales of these strange waters. They believed that all the wrecks and derelicts of the Atlantic eventually drift to the vast pool of weed and there hopelessly tangle in a mat of vegetation, slowly eddy, round and round in desolate assembly, until time and shipworms rot their hulks and send them to the bottom.

Artists and romancers have exercised their imaginations, even to the fantastic picture of a vast vortex—the later lost ships at the outside, toward the middle old pirate vessels, and in the very center Phoenician galleys still afloat on a voyage which has no end.

Sea lore taught them that the Sargasso Sea was indeed the "Port of Missing Ships," the "Ocean Graveyard," or "Davy Jones's Locker," for under the sluggish weeds were Greek triremes, Portuguese caravels, and Spanish galleons.

The medieval mariner peopled the Sargasso with strange monsters and related tales of immense octopi, which rose out of its uncanny depths to drag down with their huge tentacles unfortunate vessels entangled in the weed.

In olden times, sailors believed that the entire Sargasso was filled with weeds and that a ship might be lost forever by being caught in gigantic seaweed growths; and of crews becoming paralyzed by the breathless air, until they died of suffocation or hunger.

Until disillusioning scholars plumbed all the depths of the "Sea of Darkness," scores of unsolved mysteries of the sea had been attributed to the Sargasso.

Dreamers have long imagined that somewhere among the seaweed of the Sargasso Sea was to be found the lost continent of Atlantis.

Atlantis was the creation of old and inaccurate chroniclers who gathered and warped miscellaneous data of history and physical phenomena. The stories of the powerful capital, as outlined by the Greek philospher Plato, are widely considered to be pure fabrication, fiction, and folklore.

It was told that Atlantis was a huge island in the sea west of Gibraltar. This dream country, the thread of whose legend may be traced through the folklore and priestcraft of a dozen countries, was thought to occupy most of the space where the Atlantic now lies. Thousands of years ago, the armies of this rich and powerful happy land had dominated much of North Africa and

Western Europe, but the Greeks had halted their march of conquest.

Suddenly an upheaval of nature overwhelmed the country by an onrushing sea, causing the entire island-continent to sink beneath the waves. This is supposed to be the origin of the Flood story, which is so curiously and inexplicably universal.

Ancient accounts of this island have stimulated men's imaginations for centuries, inspiring extensive scientific research of the Sargasso Sea in modern times.

Now that both poles have been conquered, and men have scaled Mt. Everest, and Africa and Australia have ceased to be unknown continents, scientists are planning explorations to the very floor of the seas.

Man has eliminated the mermaid and merman, but has confirmed the wildest imaginations of sea serpents in the existence of the giant octopus. He has discovered stranger deep-sea fishes than even a drug-stimulated hallucination could conceive.

We know now that no ship need fear permanent entanglement in the Sargasso Sea, and that in this "Port of Missing Ships" man can expect to find nothing more than a few bits of debris, such as might be seen on any other part of the ocean. It is merely a comparatively quiet spot, the hub of a huge, vaguely defined circle of seaweed, the spawning ground of the common eel.

Far from being the region of dread pictured by medieval mariners, the Sargasso Sea is to men of natural history, oceanography, botany, and geology a paradise of strange and fascinating rewards.

It is indeed a wonderful area, and we must marvel at the courage of Columbus, who led his crews across this mysterious, trackless, seemingly treacherous area.

Professional seamen who regularly cruise to Bermuda, which lies in the middle of this sea of weeds, must smile when a novice and apprehensive seaman asks about the weird stories of the Sargasso Sea.

# VII

## Latest Losses
and
a Theory

# Loss of the Scorpion

The nuclear-powered submarine, U.S.S. *Scorpion,* valued at $40 million, disappeared with its entire crew of 99 officers and enlisted men while en route home to the United States after a Mediterranean training operation in May 1968.

An extensive search was conducted, and on October 29, some 10,000 feet deep and 460 miles southwest of the Azores, her wreckage was located.

A court of inquiry report released in January 1969 summarized that, despite 12,000 photographs of Atlantic floor debris, the U.S. Navy is still unable to say what happened to the sub.

After hearing 90 witnesses and piling up 1,334 pages of testimony during 11 weeks, the 7-man court of inquiry said, "The certain cause of the loss of *Scorpion* cannot be ascertained from any evidence now available."

The *Scorpion* is the worst submarine disaster since the *Thresher* was crushed after a piping failure off New England in 1963.

## More Losses

Lloyds Shipping Exchange in London disclosed that between June 30, 1969 and July 10, 1969, four abandoned boats were found unmanned in the "Limbo of the Lost."

June 30, 1969: No survivors could be found by the crew of the British ship *Maplebank* after coming in contact with an abandoned, 60-foot vessel several hundred miles northeast of Bermuda.

July 6, 1969: *The Vagabond,* a 20-foot fiberglass boat was found by the Swedish ship *Golar Frost.* A boarding party discovered everything on board undisturbed but no sign of the crew. The last entry in the boat's log was July 2, 1969.

July 8, 1969: A 36-foot craft was found crewless between the Azores and Bermuda by the British tanker *Helisoma.* Nothing could be found in the area to tell why the crew abandoned her.

July 10, 1969: U.S. Air Force planes abandoned search for the crew of a deserted 41-foot, 3-hulled (trimoran) yacht *Teignmouth Electronic.* She was found between the Azores and Bermuda. The board of inquiry could not come up with any realistic answer, but it was pointed out that the disappearance happened during a period of extremely calm weather.

A Lloyds' spokesman stated, "It's rare to get reports like these in such a close area in such a vast ocean. It is rather odd." No weather phenomena or gale force conditions existed in any of the cited cases.

August 14, 1969: A 20-foot craft, *Brendan the Bold,*

disappeared 400 miles northeast of Puerto Rico. The captain of the vessel, Bill Verity, was an expert seaman. In 1966, Verity crossed the Atlantic in a 12-foot boat, alone.

November 4, 1969: The yacht *Southern Cross* was discovered near Hereford Inlet, approximately 10 miles northeast of Cape May, New Jersey. The boat was reportedly on its way to Maryland and then was scheduled to head for the Bahamas. The Coast Guard gave up the hunt without coming up with the slightest answer as to why the vessel had been abandoned.

October 31, 1971: A radio equipped, 25-foot fishing vessel, *Lucky Edur,* was found by a Coast Guard patrol boat just off the coast of New Jersey. The strange part is that the ignition switch was still on, the clutch still engaged, the throttle wide open, and yet not one person was on board. There was no gasoline in the tank and all ten life preservers were hanging in place, still intact. The sea conditions were excellent, winds were light, no fog, and the water temperature 62.8 degrees. To this day, only speculation exists as to what happened to the entire crew. I have my opinion. What do you think?

February 14, 1972: Ship wreckage was spotted by sonar in the Gulf of Mexico and identified by divers as the 572-foot tanker *V. A. Fogg.* The tanker was reported missing with 39 crew members aboard after leaving Freeport, Texas, February 1, on a mission to clean out 2 tanks of xylene at approximately 50 miles offshore. After the cleaning operation, the *Fogg* was scheduled to return to Galveston, Texas. No radio contact from the vessel was received after it left port. A Coast Guard spokesman in Washington, D.C., stated that they could not say for sure what happened to 38

of the 39 men aboard. The only body found was that of
the ship's captain. The hair-raising part of this mystery is the fact that the captain was discovered sitting
in his cabin still clutching his coffee cup. What could
have caused the *V. A. Fogg* to go down so fast that
the radio man could not have sent an automatic SOS?
Thirty-eight crewmen could not launch life saving gear?
What could strike so fast that the captain's life was
snuffed out without warning. The answer is, "nothing
of this world."

# An Interview with the Author

Following is an interview between John Wallace
Spencer and Bantam's editor, in which the author dis-
cusses his own theory about the "Limbo of the Lost."
It is printed specially for this edition of the book.

BANTAM: Mr. Spencer, we would like to ask you
some questions regarding your own personal opinions
and conclusions regarding this area of disappearance.
In the first place, why do you call it the "Limbo of the
Lost" instead of the "Bermuda Triangle"?

SPENCER: The original research article released in
1964 indicated that all losses took place within a triangle which could be made by drawing a line from Miami
to Puerto Rico, then to Bermuda and back again to Miami. When the submarine *Scorpion* disappeared, my
original belief was that the *Scorpion*'s disappearance
was connected with this region. But, after careful research, I uncovered the fact that the tragedy was one
that could definitely be explained. There are thousands
of photographs of debris that can be identified with

the *Scorpion*. We were searching the whole area and were tipped off by the Russians, who were aware where the *Scorpion* had last been located through their own tracking. At this point I started my own research about the area.

BANTAM: And what did you find?

SPENCER: I noted that some of the stories were in error—notably the report that two KC-135 tankers had disappeared with all crew members. Actually, the two planes had crashed into one another. This caused me to examine in greater detail the area I call the "Limbo of the Lost."

BANTAM: How does this area differ from the so-called "Triangle"?

SPENCER: By taking all the losses and plotting them on a map, I concluded that the boundary of the area goes straight out from Cape May, New Jersey to the edge of the continental shelf. It follows the continental shelf south around Florida, through the Florida Straits, into the Gulf of Mexico, continues through the Antilles and up again, including a 440-mile circumference around Bermuda.

BANTAM: Why did you choose the name "Limbo of the Lost" for this whole area?

SPENCER: Because *limbo* is a state of existence that is neither here nor there—according to the dictionary, "a region or condition of oblivion." Ships, planes, and people simply cannot disappear with such frequency without leaving a clue as to what has occurred.

BANTAM: In your book you have quoted many suggested theories. Which one do you personally favor?

SPENCER: None of them.

BANTAM: Do you mean that you have a completely different explanation?

SPENCER: When you get involved in a mystery like the one I have been researching, you find yourself at the crossroads.

One direction takes me into science fiction, in which I do not believe. The other is reality. I am a realist.

I know, through extensive research, that unidentified flying objects do indeed exist and that the number of reported documented sightings, those reported entering or leaving the water in the "Limbo of the Lost" area, cannot be paralleled in any other part of the world.

According to all such reports, from Biblical times to the present date, two distinct types of extraterrestrial craft have been constantly observed and recorded; one type being the famous "flying saucer"—about 80 feet in circumference—and the other being of size unknown but able to carry 12 to 25 saucers inside. This is the often reported "cigar-shaped" or cylindrical object—a gigantic aircraft carrier.

Since a 575-foot vessel with 39 crew members disappearing 50 miles offshore in the Gulf of Mexico, and commercial airliners disappearing while coming in for a landing cannot happen according to earthly standards and yet *are* happening, I am forced to conclude that they are actually being taken away from our planet for a variety of reasons.

I am devoting my present efforts not to a continuous documentation of these disappearances but to ascertaining the reasons behind them and their importance to us all.

## ABOUT THE AUTHOR

JOHN WALLACE SPENCER, born in Boston, Massachusetts, in 1934, is a man of diversified interests and has been an UFOlogist for much of his life. During a ten-year stint in the U.S. Air Force, one of his jobs was to report all UFO activity to the Wright-Patterson Air Force Base. He also is a former investigator for the National Investigations Committee on Aerial Phenomena. Research, history, writing, acting, and UFO investigation are among his hobbies.

Mr. Spencer became interested in the "Limbo of the Lost" area when the nuclear submarine *Scorpion* disappeared in the Atlantic with its crew of 99 men. Through his research, a fascinating pattern began to unfold, compelling him to dig further into the subject. Mr. Spencer lives in Springfield, Massachusetts, with his wife and three children. He also lectures for the Bantam Lecture Bureau.

# Author of LIMBO OF THE LOST,

# JOHN WALLACE SPENCER

## Leaves Audiences Spellbound

In January, 1969, John Wallace Spencer appeared on a TV talkshow to discuss the mysterious disappearances of more than 100 ships and planes in the area of the mid-Atlantic known as THE BERMUDA TRIANGLE and THE DEVIL'S TRIANGLE. Following the broadcast, the station was swamped with calls; listeners, bookstores and libraries created an overwhelming demand for Mr. Spencer's book—and for Mr. Spencer.

Former member of the world-famous NATIONAL INVESTIGATION COMMITTEE ON AERIAL PHENOMENA, John Wallace Spencer spent 10 years in the U.S. Air Force, was a newspaper editor, teacher and TV and radio announcer. His provocative lectures and stimulating question and answer period leave audiences of every age and sex literally spellbound!

Mr. Spencer is available for speaking engagements through the BANTAM LECTURE BUREAU. For further details, contact:

# RELAX!

## SIT DOWN
## and Catch Up On Your Reading!

# OTHER WORLDS.
# OTHER REALITIES.

In fact and fiction, these extraordinary books bring the fascinating world of the supernatural down to earth. From ancient astronauts and black magic to witchcraft, voodoo and mysticism—these books look at other worlds and examine other realities.

- [ ] **CHARIOTS OF THE GODS (Q5753/$1.25)—Fact**
- [ ] **THE EXORCIST (X7200/$1.75)—Fiction**
- [ ] **WITCHCRAFT AND BLACK MAGIC (R6836/$1.45)—Fact**
- [ ] **RAGA SIX (Q7249/$1.25)—Fiction**
- [ ] **POWER THROUGH WITCHCRAFT (N5713/95¢)—Fact**
- [ ] **HELL HOUSE (N7277/95¢)—Fiction**
- [ ] **I CHING (Q5214/$1.25)—Fact**
- [ ] **A COMPLETE GUIDE TO THE TAROT (Q6696/$1.25)—Fact**
- [ ] **GODS FROM OUTER SPACE (Q7276/$1.25)—Fact**

# WE DELIVER!
## And So Do These Bestsellers.

# FREE!
## Bantam Book Catalog

It lists over a thousand money-saving bestsellers originally priced from $3.75 to $15.00 —bestsellers that are yours now for as little as 50¢ to $2.25!

The catalog gives you a great opportunity to build your own private library at huge savings!

So don't delay any longer—send for your catalog TODAY! It's absolutely FREE!

# PSYCHIC WORLD

*Here are some of the leading books that delve into the world of the occult—that shed light on the powers of prophecy, of reincarnation and of foretelling the future.*